English Code 5

Activity Book

Contents

Welcome! .... p. 6

1 Time for school .... p. 10

2 Landscapes of China .... p. 22

    Checkpoint 1 .... p. 34
    Culture 1 .... p. 36

3 Hanging out .... p. 38

4 Cinema magic .... p. 50

    Checkpoint 2 .... p. 62
    Culture 2 .... p. 64

5 Once in a lifetime .... p. 66

6 Codes and clues .... p. 78

    Checkpoint 3 .... p. 90
    Culture 3 .... p. 92

7 What shall we eat? .... p. 94

8 Our digital world .... p. 106

    Checkpoint 4 .... p. 118
    Culture 4 .... p. 120
    Extra writing pages .... p. 122

OUR WORLD

INTRO:
Here we stand: children of every age,
This is our world and the world's our stage.
We can laugh, we can cry — we can float, we can fly,
We can dance, we can sing — we can do almost anything
in OUR world … our *beautiful* world.

VERSE 1:
Some of us are small; some of us are tall,
Some of us are shy; some say hi to everybody,
Some of us like numbers; some of us love words,
Some of us watch football, and some of us watch the birds!

(CHORUS)
This is our world … we're different but the same.
We live and learn together — we get to know each other …
in OUR world … our *beautiful* world.

VERSE 2:
Some of us like music; some of us like cars,
Some of us draw pictures, looking at the stars,
Some of us are scientists, trying to find the code,
All of us can help a friend and give a hand to hold.

This is our world — there's room for everyone.
We learn to live together, and we have a lot of fun …
In **our** world … in **our** world … in our beautiful world!

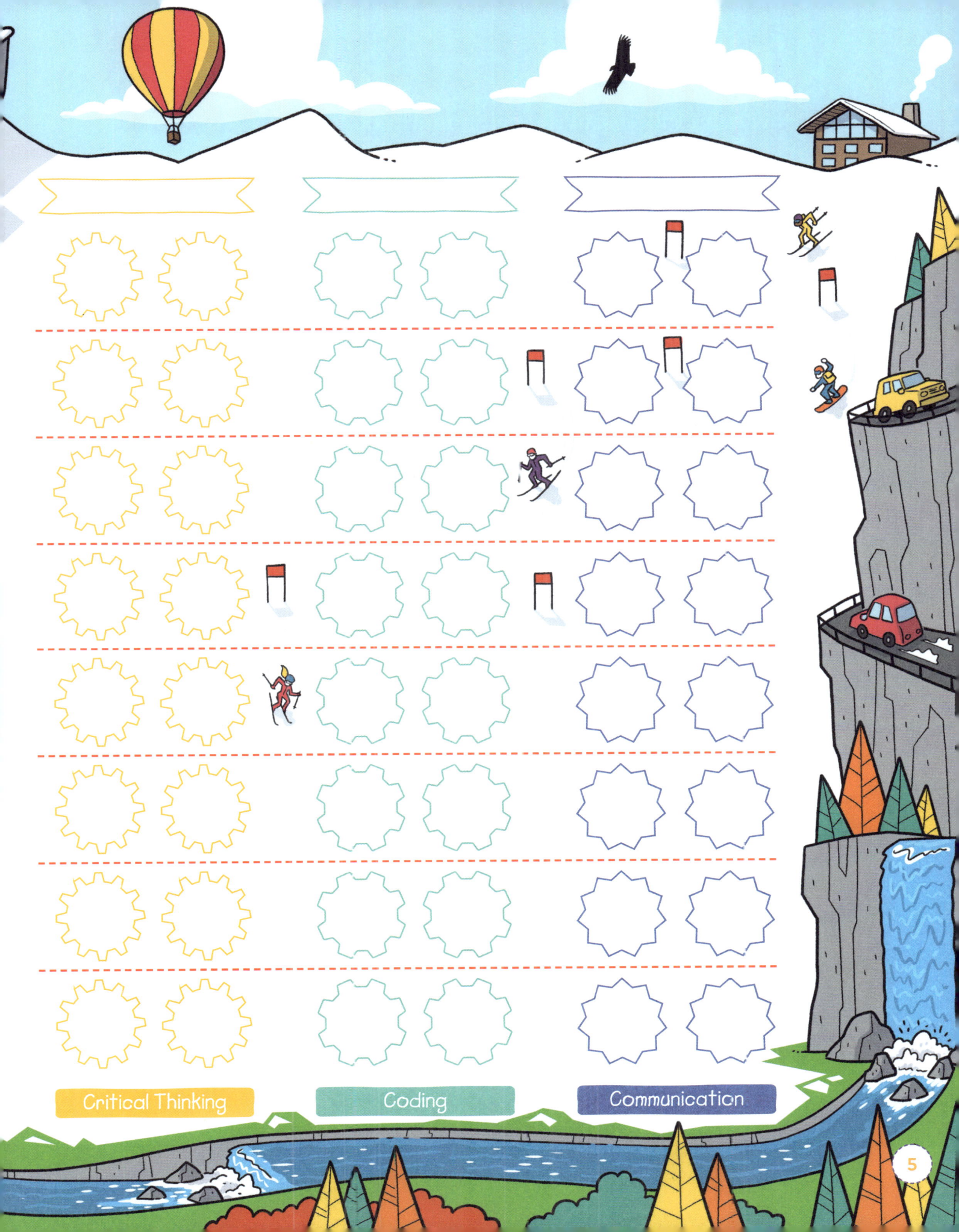

Welcome!

How can I talk about my neighbourhood?

1 Look at Pupil's Book page 5. Create your own *Neighbour of the Month* fact file.

2 Read and complete. Then listen and check.

boxes   hobbies   lives   name   world

People in my neighbourhood have got interesting **1** _____ . Our neighbour, Mrs Drake, collects plates. She brings them from all over the **2** _____ . Have you got a neighbour with interesting hobbies?

Another neighbour, Mr Green, is very friendly and helps with things like carrying heavy **3** _____ . Have you got friendly neighbours?

My best friend **4** _____ at number 24. Her **5** _____ is Abby. I go to her house at the weekends to play board games. Have you got a friend who lives near you?

3 Complete the sequences.

CODE CRACKER

a 2 ____ 6 8 ____ ____ 14
b 3 5 ____ ____ 11 13 ____
c 72 82 92 ____ 112 ____
d 99 ____ 95 ____ 91 ____

4 Play *Word Categories – Stop!*

A first name:	A surname:	A hobby:	Furniture in a house:	A place:
Fred	Fernandez	fishing	fridge	farm

6

Our neighbourhood

VOCABULARY

> I will talk about people and places in my neighbourhood.

1 Read the definitions and write the words.

1. a fun name that people call you   _____
2. the name your parents gave you   _____
3. the name you share with other family members   _____
4. the people who live near you   _____

2 Read about where Jenny lives. Then complete the table.

I live in a block of flats with a great view. I can see mountains and trees from my window. But our flat is small and noisy. I haven't got my own room and can't get away from my sisters.

One good thing about our building is the neighbours are friendly. If we need something, we can ask for help.

There is a small supermarket and a bus stop on our street. Mum says it is convenient for going into town.

Our neighbourhood is nice, but there aren't many parks. It's a little bit boring for children.

Good things	Bad things
It's got a great view.	It's small and noisy.

3 Complete the table about where you live.

Things you like	Things you don't like
_____	_____
_____	_____
_____	_____
_____	_____
_____	_____

4 Complete the sentences.

> blended family   housewarming party
> removals workers   residence

1. The place where I live is my _____.

2. I've got a dad, a stepmum, a stepbrother and two half-sisters. We are a _____.

3. Would you like to come over to our house? There will be music and food. We are having a _____.

4. People who pack your things and take them to your new house are called _____.

I can talk about people and places in my neighbourhood.

Language lab 1

GRAMMAR: -WHERE, -ONE, -THING

I will learn to use general words, e.g., everywhere, everyone, everything.

1 Read and complete.

> anywhere   everyone   everything   everywhere   somewhere

My Well-Travelled Neighbour

My neighbour Tony has been almost **1** _____ in the world! He loves talking about his travels and telling **2** _____ about his adventures. Before Tony goes **3** _____ new, he reads all about the place on the internet. He likes to know **4** _____ about the place before he goes. Where would you go if you could go **5** _____ ?

2  **Now listen and check your answers.**

3 Unscramble the words and complete the sentences.

> oaynne   onnthig   wynreahe   ythaning

1. Is there _____ good to eat in your fridge?
2. Is there _____ good to eat in your town?
3. Do you know _____ who rides a motorbike to school?
4. What day of the week do you like to relax and do _____ ?

4 In pairs, ask and answer the questions in 3.

5 Read and solve the maths problem.

MATHS ZONE

There are 36 people on my street. One third are women, one third are men and one third are children. Of the children, half are girls. How many boys live on our street?

_____

I can use general words, e.g., everywhere , everyone , everything .

Story lab
READING

I will read a story about getting to know neighbours.

1 Read, look at the pictures and match.

1. Tom looked out of the window and saw Hoops and Rebecca waving at him. He did know someone at the street party!
2. 'Wait!' said Hoops. 'My first name is Peter, but my nickname is Hoops. People usually call me Hoops because I love basketball.'
   Tom gave the letter to Hoops.
3. First, Tom tried flat 302. A girl opened the door. Her name wasn't Peter Adams; it was Rebecca Williams.

2 Write the answers. Then ask and answer in pairs.

1. Did you live in the same house last year or have you moved recently?
   _____
2. Is there anyone new on your street or in your block of flats?
   _____
3. Are you or is anyone else new at school this year?
   _____
4. How can you be kind to a new person at school?
   _____
5. Do you like meeting new people?
   _____

3 Listen and write.

A: What's your name?
B: I'm **1** _____ . How about you?
A: I'm **2** _____ . What's your surname, Nick?
B: My surname is **3** _____ . And yours?
A: My surname is **4** _____ . Nice to meet you, **5** _____ !
B: Nice to meet you, **6** _____ !

4 Practise the conversation in 3 with a partner. Use your names.

5 What do you do when you meet someone new? Tick  .

In my country, we smile at each other. ☐
In my country, we bow. ☐
In my country, we shake hands. ☐

 read a story about getting to know neighbours.

1 Time for school
How do we design our ideal school?

1 Read and sort.

books   flowers   gardening   learn   lesson   model   open-air   playground   trees   vegetables

Classroom	Greenhouse	Outside

2 Solve the maths problems to find the secret message. Use the code.

CODE CRACKER

1	2	3	4	5	6	7	8	9	10	11	12	13	14	15	16
a	e	i	o	u	b	c	f	j	m	n	r	s	t	v	l

___ ___ ___ ___ ___ ___ ___ ___ ___ ___ ___ ___ ___
12÷4 4x4 10–6 9+6 10÷5 9+4 11–4 12÷4 14÷7 6+5 4+3 14–12

3 Read and complete. Then listen and check your answers.

grow   look after   make   read   water

In gardening class, we **1** _____ books about how to **2** _____ flowers and plants and **3** _____ vegetables. Then we go outside and do some gardening! When it's hot, we **4** _____ the flowers and vegetables more frequently using a new watering system. I'm going to **5** _____ a model of the watering system and give a presentation about how it works.

4 What outdoor activities do you do at school? Ask and answer.

I plant things.   I do experiments.   I tidy up.

School life

VOCABULARY

I will learn words to describe education and learning.

1 Circle the odd one out.

1. lunch / experiment / equipment
2. bag / pyjamas / lunch box
3. make a model / do a test / make your bed
4. outside / headteacher / classmate
5. inside / football field / playground

2 Listen, read and circle T (True) or F (False).

1. Harry's talking about his English class. T / F
2. He's making a model volcano. T / F
3. Sally likes Maths. T / F
4. She's got a test on addition and subtraction. T / F
5. In Helen's favourite class, they only do painting. T / F

3 Complete the sentences.

equipment   model   outside   practise   uniform

1. If you want to be good at playing the piano, you need to _____ every day.
2. I love going _____ at break.
3. When you design things, it's a good idea to draw pictures or make a _____ .
4. Some children wear a _____ at school.
5. You usually need special _____ when you do a Science experiment.

4 Listen and label the pictures.

certificate   dictionary   exam   goggles

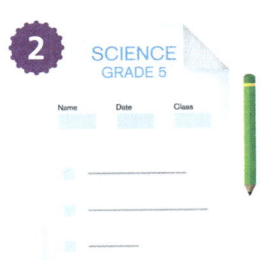

_____   _____

_____   _____

5 Say the tongue twisters as quickly as you can.

a. I think I'll drink a pink drink on Thursday.
b. Some silly swinging monkeys are singing songs.

I can use words to describe education and learning.

Language lab

GRAMMAR: EXPRESSING RULES WITH *MUST*

I will express rules using **must** and **mustn't**.

1 Read and circle the correct words.

1. You **must** / **mustn't** touch any of the objects in the museum.
2. You **must** / **mustn't** bring bags into the museum.
3. The museum closes at 6:00 p.m. You **must** / **mustn't** leave at 5:45 p.m.
4. No animals allowed. You **must** / **mustn't** come into the museum with pets.
5. No photos allowed. You **must** / **mustn't** take photos.

2 Complete the rules with must or mustn't. Then write G (Gym), L (Library) or S (Science lab).

  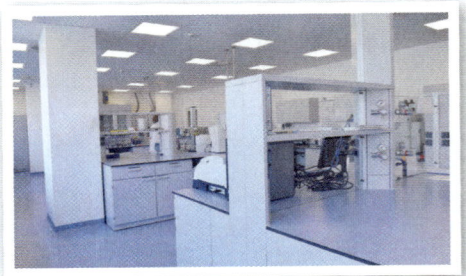

1. You _____ wear sports clothes to play volleyball. ___
2. You _____ wash and put away equipment after you do an experiment. ___
3. You _____ eat or drink on the basketball court. ___
4. You _____ take your books back before the return date. ___
5. You _____ remove the magazines from the reading area. ___
6. You _____ listen to the safety instructions when you do an experiment. ___

3 Make a poster with class rules using must/mustn't.

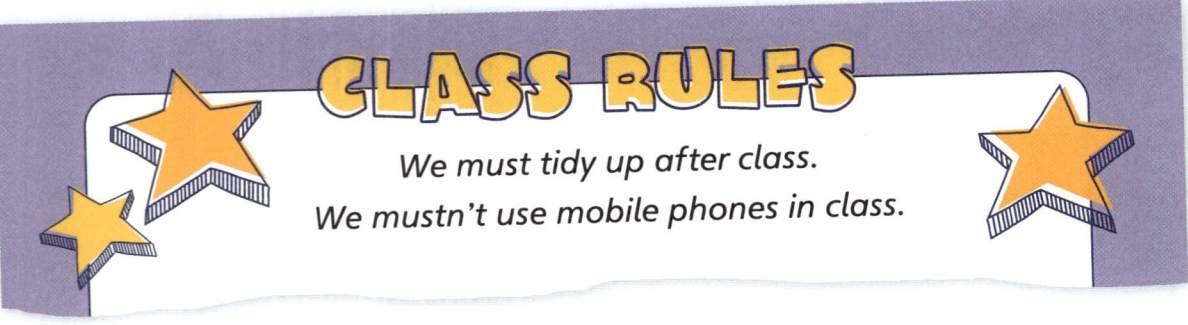

CLASS RULES

We must tidy up after class.
We mustn't use mobile phones in class.

Values Think about rules.

4 Listen and number. Write a rule for each photo.

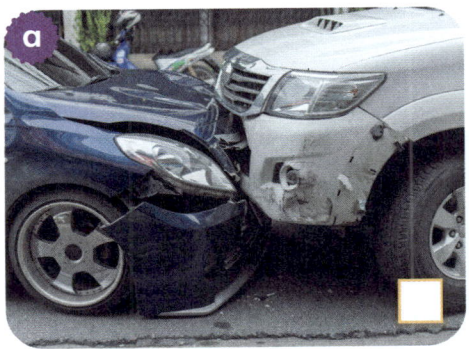  

stop / red light   clean up / after pets   drop / litter

1 _____
2 _____
3 _____

5 Read the article and write the rules below.

WORLD'S BIGGEST MAZE

Do you know where the world's largest maze is located? It's in China and it's called the *Dream Maze*. There are many different paths in the *Dream Maze*. The walls of the paths are tall hedges.

There are resting places inside the maze. There's a lot of walking to do inside the maze and people can get tired. It's a good idea to wear the right clothes and strong shoes because the paths have got rocks and stones. There's no water inside the maze, so it's important to bring a bottle of water. Most importantly, don't lose your family and friends in the maze, especially your children.

The maze opens at 10 a.m. and closes at 5 p.m. Don't leave anyone inside the maze!

1 (wear walking shoes) _____
2 (bring water) _____
3 (watch your children) _____
4 (leave at 5 p.m.) _____
5 (forget anyone) _____

I can express rules using must and mustn't.

Story lab
READING

> I will read a story about robots in a school.

THE ROBOT HELPERS

1 Read the beginning and the end of *The Robot Helpers* and complete the sentences.

> When I was 11, our school headteacher was a woman called Mrs Miller. She was crazy about computers and robots. One morning, she said, 'I've got a surprise for you. Meet our amazing new robots. They're here to help us!'
>
> The robots couldn't open the doors, so they couldn't go outside. They moved more and more slowly, and finally, they stopped. Mrs Miller took out their batteries and we were all happy!
>
> …
>
> 'Thanks, kids', said Mrs Miller. 'I'm not keen on robots now!'

1 Mrs Miller was the _____ of the school.
2 She liked _____ in the beginning.
3 In the end, Mrs Miller took out the robots' _____ .
4 She _____ keen on robots in the end.

2 Circle the things in the story.

computers	cats	robots	surprise	breakfast
homework	equipment	the world	the football field	floor
bedroom	screen	message	solar panels	power
keys	doors	outside	batteries	

14

3 Number the sentences in order.

a *First*, Mrs Miller brought robots to school to help the students. ____
b *Suddenly*, the robots wanted to take over the world, destroy the classrooms and make more robots. ____
c *Then* the students saw the low battery and locked the doors so the robots couldn't recharge their batteries in the sunlight. ____
d *Then* the robots helped the children with their work and carried equipment. ____
e *Finally*, the robots stopped, Mrs Miller took out the batteries and everyone was happy. ____

4 Write an alternative ending to *The Robot Helpers*.

_____
_____

5 Your headteacher has got some robots for you. Write a set of rules for your classroom robots.

_____
_____
_____

6 Write your opinion of the story.

Key
1 = very bad
5 = very good

My opinion
My favourite character is _____.
My favourite part is _____.
I think the story is interesting / funny / scary / silly .
I liked / didn't like the story because _____
_____.
I think it's _____ story. I _____ and _____.

❶   ❷   ❸   ❹   ❺

I can read a story about robots in a school.

Experiment lab
SCIENCE: LIGHT AND LIGHT ENERGY

I will find out which surfaces reflect or absorb light.

1 Read and complete.

> artificial light   Electric lights   natural light   rays   reflects   Solar   torch

Light Quiz

The Sun is important because it gives us natural light. Natural light from the Sun _____ off the Moon. That reflection is what we see in the night sky. The Moon does not produce light. The Sun's _____ travel through space to warm our planet. Solar power production takes the Sun's rays and turns them into electricity. _____ panels absorb heat from the Sun to capture its energy and turn it into electricity. The Sun is the only source of _____ .

Light that is not natural is called _____ . An example of artificial light is a _____ . It gets its energy from a battery, not the Sun. _____ are another example of artificial light. We use them to light our homes, offices and streets.

2 Match to make sentences.

1 Candles are
2 Rays from the Sun
3 Solar panels
4 The Sun gives us
5 The Moon

a natural light.
b absorb light and turn it into energy.
c shine down and warm our planet.
d a form of artificial light.
e reflects the Sun's light.

3 Read and solve the maths problem.

MATHS ZONE

There has been a power cut. All the houses on Ana's street need light. Each house needs one candle per room.
House 1: six rooms   House 4: eight rooms
House 2: five rooms   House 5: nine rooms
House 3: seven rooms
How many candles should Ana buy to light the street?
_____

EXPERIMENT TIME

Report

1 Look and label the pictures.

> aluminium foil   black paper   desk   jumper   light-coloured paper   wooden door

1. _____
2. _____
3. _____
4. _____
5. _____
6. _____

2 Look at **1** again. Tick ✓ the surfaces that reflected light well in your experiment.

3 Think about <u>your</u> experiment. Complete the table.

Materials that absorbed light	Materials that reflected light
_____	_____
_____	_____
_____	_____

4 Write your report.

Reflect or absorb?
White paper: White paper reflects light.

Black paper: Black paper _____ light.
Aluminium foil: Aluminium foil _____ light.
_____ : _____ reflects light.
_____ : _____ absorbs light.
_____ : _____ _____ light.

I know which surfaces reflect or absorb light.

A friend in India

COMMUNICATION

*I will talk about obligations using **have to** and **don't have to**.*

1 🎧 **Listen to an interview with Karen and tick ✓ the information about her.**

1. ☐ a Karen plays the piano. ☐ b Karen plays the drums.
2. ☐ a She has to practise once a week. ☐ b She has to practise every day.
3. ☐ a She has to do exams. ☐ b She doesn't have to do exams.
4. ☐ a She has to wear special clothes. ☐ b She doesn't have to wear special clothes.
5. ☐ a She has to use a special chair. ☐ b She has to use a song book.

2 💬 **Complete the questions. Then choose a role and ask and answer.**

Interviewer: What sports or activities **1** _____ you do?
Interviewer: Do you **2** _____ practise every day?
Interviewer: Do you have to do **3** _____ or tests?
Interviewer: Do you have to **4** _____ a uniform or special clothes?
Interviewer: **5** _____ _____ have to use special equipment?

EMILY
- **Sport:** volleyball
- **Practise:** on Monday and Wednesday
- **Exams or tests:** no
- **Uniform:** yes, team uniform
- **Special equipment:** volleyball, volleyball net

TERESA
- **Activity:** go to Art class
- **Attend:** once a week
- **Practise:** yes, draw in a sketchbook every day
- **Exams or tests:** enter an exhibition once a year
- **Uniform:** a smock
- **Special equipment:** paint brushes, pencils, sketchbook

3 Complete for you. Write notes.

Name: _____ Exams or tests: _____
Activity or sport: _____ Uniform: _____
Practise: _____ Special equipment: _____

4 💬 **Ask and answer. Use the questions in 2 and the information in 3.**

 talk about obligations using **have to** and **don't have to**.

Writing lab

INSTRUCTIONS FOR A GAME

> I will write instructions for a game.

1 Circle the words you know. Use a dictionary to find the meaning of the words you don't know.

play   throw   catch   hit   pick up   roll   count   take turns   win   score   try

2 Read the instructions and answer the questions.

HOW TO PLAY — BIN BASKETBALL

EQUIPMENT: one paper ball, one clean bin

OBJECTIVE: Play in two teams. You must score more points than the other team.

HOW TO PLAY

- Each team has to take turns. You must stand three metres away from the bin. You have to throw the ball into the bin to score a point for your team.
- You must pick up the ball after your turn and give it to a person on the opposite team.
- You have to count points after everyone has a turn and keep score.
- You have to play three rounds. Count the score at the end of three rounds. The winning team is the one with the most points.

1 What equipment do you need for bin basketball? _____
2 What's the objective of the game? _____
3 Do you have to take turns? _____
4 Do you have to pick up the ball? _____

3 Read and solve the maths problems.

MATHS ZONE
I score 3 points, Mark scores 5 points, Sarah scores 3 points. How many points do we score in total?
I score 5 points. My team scores a total of 25 points. What percentage of my team's points do I score?

4 Write your own variation of *Bin basketball* in your notebook.

I can write instructions for a game.

PROJECT AND REVIEW UNIT 1

Design your ideal school

Project report

1 Complete for your ideal school.

Type of school			Holidays and homework
☐ inside	☐ outside	☐ teachers	☐ 10 weeks of holiday
☐ headteacher	☐ robots	☐ Art	☐ 15 weeks of holiday
☐ sports	☐ Maths	☐ activities	☐ some homework
☐ solar panels	☐ experiments	☐ equipment	☐ a lot of homework
☐ big	☐ small	☐ garden	

2 Complete your project report.

My School

Location:

Equipment:

Buildings:

Homework:

Design:

Holiday:

No. of teachers:

Rules:

Subjects:

Extra features:

3 Present your report to your class.

I can design my ideal school.

Review

1 Look at the rules. Write sentences with **have to**, **don't have to**, **must** or **mustn't**.

help others ✓ — We have to help others.
keep our classroom tidy ✓✓ — We must keep our classroom tidy.
wear a uniform ✗ — We don't have to wear a uniform.
be late ✗✗ — We mustn't be late.

1 study for tests ✓ _____
2 do sport at school ✗ _____
3 use mobile phones at school ✗✗ _____
4 listen to the teacher ✓✓ _____

2 Read and circle the correct words.

1 Q: **Do** / Does she have to practise every day?
   A: Yes, she have to / **has to** practise every day.
2 Q: Do / **Does** he have to do tests?
   A: No, he don't / **doesn't** have to do tests.
3 Q: **Do** / Does I have to wear a uniform?
   A: No, you do / **don't** have to wear a uniform.
4 Q: Does she have to / **has to** study Music?
   A: Yes, she have to / **has to** study Music.

3 💬 Ask and answer.

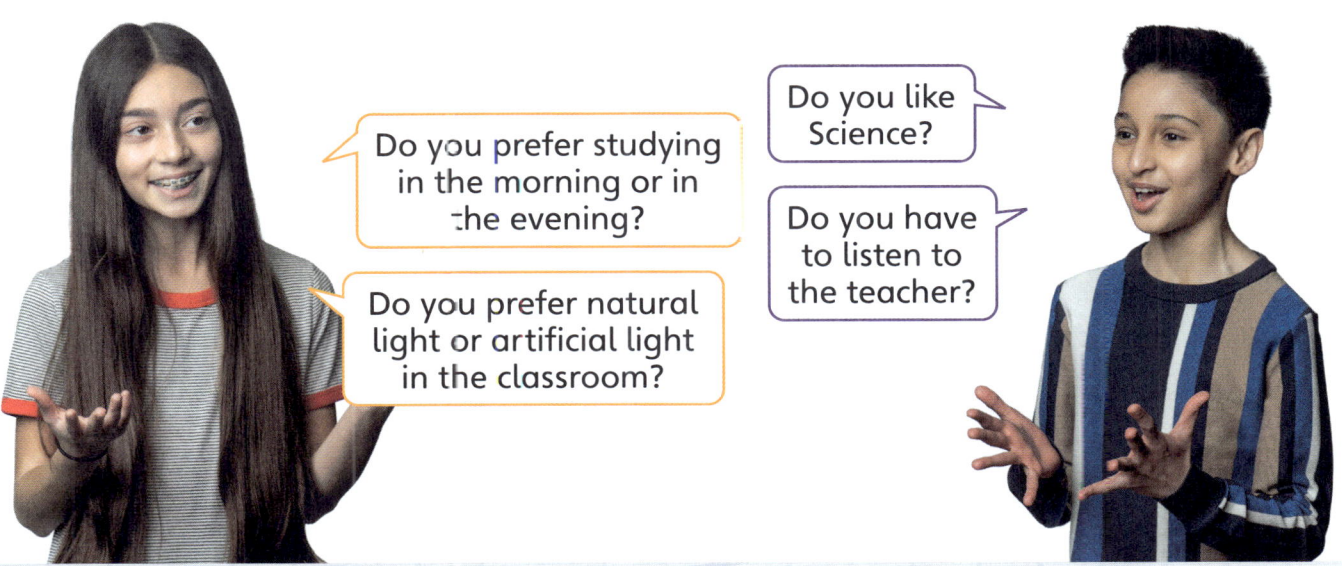

Do you prefer studying in the morning or in the evening?

Do you prefer natural light or artificial light in the classroom?

Do you like Science?

Do you have to listen to the teacher?

▶▶ Now go to your Progress Chart on page 4.

21

2 Landscapes of China

How can I make a story plate?

1 Look and write a–d. Then read and match.

1   A place with a lot of trees together.
2   Land with water all around it.
3   A high area of land, sometimes with snow on top.
4   A large area of water, with land all around it.

☐ lake
☐ forest
☐ mountain
☐ island

2 Write the code. Then use it to write the sentence.

CODE CRACKER

1	2	3	4	5																		
a	b	c																				

I was walking by the lake when …
9   19/1/23   1   4/18/1/7/15/14   9/14   20/8/5   23/1/20/5/18

_____

3 Complete the information about China with words from **1**.

1   Two thirds of China is covered in _____ .
2   Qinghai is a very large salt _____ in China.
3   There are over 250 _____ in the South China Sea.
4   There's a large bamboo _____ very near Beijing.

4  Listen and check the answers to **3**.

Beautiful landscapes

VOCABULARY

I will learn words to describe landscapes.

1 Complete the sentences.

> desert   jungle   lake
> volcano   waterfall

1 The _____ flowed from the top of the cliff down into the _____ .

2 The _____ is active and a lot of tourists visit it every year.

3 There is very little rain in the _____ and many snakes and scorpions live there.

4 A lot of monkeys and birds live up high in the trees in the _____ .

2 🎧 011 Listen and circle T (True) or F (False).

1 Nobody ever goes to the island.   T / F
2 The island is a desert.   T / F
3 There are a lot of trees on the island.   T / F
4 People hang-glide from the volcano.   T / F
5 There's a waterfall on the coast.   T / F
6 The waterfall is a popular picnic spot.   T / F

3 Correct the false statements in 2.

_____
_____
_____
_____
_____
_____

4 🎧 012 Listen and label the pictures.

> cactus   earthquake   jetty   valley

_____   _____

_____   _____

5 Ph 🎧 013 Read, listen and chant. Then say the words that rhyme in pairs.

Come to the island,
And listen to the band,
Hand in hand on the sand.
Stand on the sand,
And clap your hands.
Show the band that you're a fan.

I can use words to describe landscapes.

Language lab

GRAMMAR: QUESTIONS ABOUT THE PAST

 I will ask questions about the past.

1 Read and circle the correct question word.

1 What / Where did you go?
2 How / Who did you see there?
3 How / Who did you travel?
4 What / When did you come home?

2 Complete with the correct question word.

1 A: _____ did you go to the museum? B: I went yesterday.
2 A: _____ did you go with? B: I went with my parents.
3 A: _____ told you about the museum? B: Some friends told us about it.
4 A: _____ did you see there? B: We saw an exhibition on Ancient China.
5 A: _____ did you have lunch? B: We had lunch in the canteen.

3 Read and circle the correct words.

1 Who lent / did lend you that book?
2 What happened / did happen when the volcano erupted?
3 Who did you go / you went to the coast with?
4 Who buy / bought you that chocolate bar?
5 What did you buy / bought in the gift shop?

4 Read the story.

A Birthday Picnic

At the weekend, Shelly invited her friends to a picnic for her birthday. The picnic was in the local forest. Everyone played and had fun. They ran under the waterfall for a while.

Shelly's mum put the picnic food out on a blanket. There was chicken and salad. There was a big birthday cake as well. Then she called everyone to come and eat.

'Where's the salad?' shouted Shelly. Then the children saw the rabbits under the trees. They had the salad. They were very happy. They loved salad for lunch.

'Hurry up and eat the chicken!' said Shelly's mum.

'Mum!' shouted Shelly. 'Rover's looking at my birthday cake!' The children looked at Rover. They all loved Shelly's dog, but he was famous for stealing cake.

'Let's sing Happy Birthday quickly!' said Shelly's mum. They all laughed.

5 Write questions about the story.

1 What / they / do / last weekend?
   _____

2 Why / they / go / to the forest?
   _____

3 Who / put / food on the blanket?
   _____

4 What / they / have?
   _____

5 What / happen / to the salad?
   _____

6 Who / want / eat / cake?
   _____

7 Why / they / sing / Happy Birthday / quickly?
   _____

6 In pairs, ask and answer the questions in 5.

7 Listen and answer the questions.

1 Where did Danny go? He went to _____.
2 Who did he go with? He went with _____.
3 What happened? A bird _____.

8 Answer the questions for you.

1 Did you go to a museum last year?
   _____

2 Who did you go with?
   _____

3 What did you see?
   _____

I can ask and answer questions about the past.

Story lab

READING

I will read a story set in ancient China.

1 Complete the information about the people in the story.

Names of characters	What do we know about them?
Lian	main character, young and kind

2 Read and circle T (True) or F (False).

1 The story is set in China. T / F
2 Lian was a very happy young girl. T / F
3 She wanted to climb the mountains and see the sea. T / F
4 Lian's father said she could go away. T / F
5 Chang told Lian about the green fields and beautiful birds. T / F
6 Lian's father wanted Lian to marry Chang. T / F

3 Answer the questions.

1 Who did Lian's father want her to marry?
_____

2 Why didn't Lian like her father's suggestion?
_____

3 Who ran away with Lian?
_____

4 Where did they go?
_____

5 Why couldn't he take his daughter home?
_____

Values — Show empathy.

4 Read and tick ☑.

Lucky Chang! I'm happy for him.

Poor Chang! I'm sad for him.

1 Chang walked in the beautiful fields.
   Lucky him! ☐   Poor him! ☐
2 Lian's father said she must marry Wang, the farmer.
   Lucky her! ☐   Poor her! ☐
3 Lian and Chang became birds.
   Lucky them! ☐   Poor them! ☐

5 When you are sad, what does your body language look like? Can you identify when someone else is sad? What can you say to them?

6 Look at the picture. Tick ☑ the part of the story you think it depicts. Discuss why with a partner.

1 Lian asked her father if she could go to the mountains. ☐
2 Lian's father wanted his daughter to marry his old friend, Wang. ☐
3 Lian's father saw his daughter in the cave. ☐

7 Write your opinion of the story.

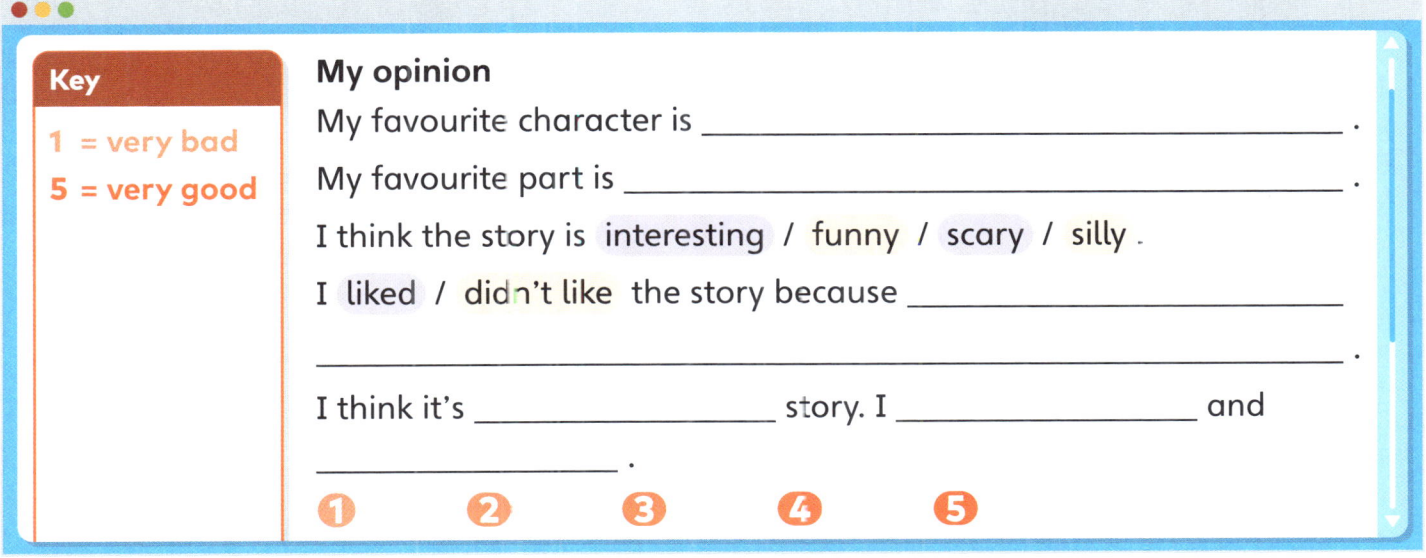

Key
1 = very bad
5 = very good

My opinion
My favourite character is _____.
My favourite part is _____.
I think the story is interesting / funny / scary / silly .
I liked / didn't like the story because _____
_____.
I think it's _____ story. I _____ and
_____.

① ② ③ ④ ⑤

I can read a story set in ancient China.

Experiment lab

SCIENCE: THE WATER CYCLE

I will find out about the water cycle.

1 Look and write.

h_____   m_____   r_____

r_____   s_____   s_____

2 Match to make sentences.

1 Water vapour rises from   a into drops of liquid.
2 Water vapour condenses   b repeats itself.
3 Drops of liquid water   c from the clouds.
4 Rain, snow or hail falls   d form into clouds or mist.
5 Finally the rain, snow or hail   e rivers, lakes and seas.
6 The whole cycle   f returns to the lakes, rivers and seas.

3 Read and complete.

> clouds   cools   cycle   hail   vapour

The water **1** _____ describes how water turns into water **2** _____ and rises from lakes, rivers and seas. The Sun heats the water and that forms the water vapour. When the air **3** _____ , the vapour turns into drops of water and forms **4** _____ . When the clouds are big and heavy, the liquid water falls as rain, snow or **5** _____ .

4 Describe what happened in your rain cloud experiment.

- I added two drops and …
- Then I added more drops and …
- I added more drops and …
- The stage of the rain cycle I saw was …

5 Think about your rain cloud experiment and complete the table.

What I already knew about rain before the experiment	What I learnt about rain during the experiment	What I still want to know about rain
I already knew that …	I learnt that …	I still want to know …

6 Answer the questions.

1. What will the weather be like in your area tomorrow?
   _____

2. Does it rain much where you live?
   _____

3. Are there any mountains in your area?
   _____

4. Are there any rivers?
   _____

5. Do you live near a lake?
   _____

I know about the water cycle.

China past and present

COMMUNICATION

I will ask questions about what life was like in the past.

1 What do people in China often have for breakfast? Tick ✓.

rice ☐   noodles ☐   toast ☐   eggs ☐   beef ☐   dumplings ☐   fruit ☐
pancakes ☐   vegetables ☐   milk ☐   soya milk ☐   orange juice ☐

2 Read and check your answers in **1**.

The Chinese invented chopsticks 4000 years ago in Henan Province. They made the first chopsticks out of twigs. They used them for stirring food in the cooking pot. Later, the Chinese began to use chopsticks to eat their food at the table. There were knives in China before chopsticks, but Confucius, the famous Chinese philosopher, was a vegetarian. He didn't want to use knives at the table.

Did you know that Chinese people use chopsticks to eat breakfast, too? What do the Chinese eat for breakfast nowadays with their chopsticks? Most people have fried rice, fried noodles, beef, dumplings, pancakes or vegetables. They drink milk, soya milk or orange juice.

3 Read the article again and answer the questions.

1. Who invented chopsticks?
   _____
   _____

2. When did they invent them?
   _____
   _____

3. What did they first use them for?
   _____
   _____

4. Which philosopher said you shouldn't use knives at the table?
   _____
   _____

4 Solve the maths problems. **MATHS ZONE**

1. Confucius was born in 551 BCE and died in 479 BCE. How long did he live?
   _____

2. The Ming Dynasty started in 1368 and ended in 1644. How long did it last?
   _____

3. Matt bought four Chinese plates: a small plate for ¥120, two matching plates for ¥275 each and a large plate for ¥525. He also bought a small vase for ¥150. How much did Matt spend in total?
   _____

I can ask questions about what life was like in the past.

Writing lab

SHAPE POEMS

I will write a shape poem.

1 Complete the shape poem.

drops   forest   tall   tree   waterfall

The _____ in the _____ is big, green and _____.
It drips excitedly with _____ from a great _____.
Sp
la
sh!

2 Read the poem again and draw a picture to illustrate it.

3 Create a shape poem called *The Lake*. You can use any of the words from the box to help you.

big   blue   dangerous   moving   river
rocks   scary   splash   streams   water

The Lake

4 Tick ✓ the things you find in your poem. Write the words.

colour ☐ _____
size   ☐ _____
feelings ☐ _____
sound   ☐ _____
action ☐ _____

5 Read your poem to the class. Listen to the other poems.

I can write a shape poem.

PROJECT AND REVIEW UNIT 2

Make a story plate

Project report

1 Complete the table for your story plate.

Who was your story about?		Where was your story set?		
☐ main character ☐ boy		☐ lake	☐ mountain	☐ island
☐ girl ☐ animal		☐ cave	☐ stream	☐ forest
other characters _____		☐ city	☐ town	☐ village
What was the problem?		**What happened?**	**What parts did you paint?**	
☐ parents	☐ friends	☐ beginning	☐ characters	☐ setting
☐ brothers	☐ sick	☐ action	☐ action	☐ beginning
☐ sisters	☐ rich	☐ ending	☐ ending	
☐ lonely	☐ poor			

2 Complete your project report.

Who was your story about?
My story was about …

Where was your story set?
It was set …

What was the problem?
The problem was …

What happened?
The main character …

What parts did you paint?
I painted …

3 Share your report with a partner. Ask questions.

I can make a story plate.

Review

1 Complete the summary with vocabulary from the unit.

My story was about pirates. It was set on Black Mountain Island, a small **1** i_____ with three **2** v_____ that erupted every year. Around the island, there was a rocky **3** c_____ with high cliffs and stony beaches. Pirates stood on the cliffs and looked for passing ships. Much of the island was covered in **4** f_____ . It was dark and full of spiders and mosquitoes. Pirates used the island to hide their treasure in a dark **5** c_____ behind a high **6** w_____ .

2 🎧 015 Listen and check your answers in **1**.

3 Answer the questions about **1**.

1 What was the story about?
   _____

2 Where was it set?
   _____

3 Which animals lived on the island?
   _____

4 What did the pirates use the island for?
   _____

5 Where did the pirates hide their treasure?
   _____

4 Complete the text with the correct form of the words. Then write the questions.

> eat   go   have   learn   see   use

I'm Holly. Last week, I _____ on a school trip with my friends. We went to a museum in town and saw an exhibition on China. We _____ some interesting information about Chinese history and _____ some beautiful painted plates and vases. We _____ lunch in the café and _____ chopsticks to eat our rice! Then, at five o'clock we got the bus home. I _____ a great day!

1 _____
   _____
   We went to a museum in town.

2 _____
   _____
   We took the bus to the museum.

3 _____
   _____
   We ate lunch in a café.

4 _____
   _____
   We went home at five o'clock.

Now go to your Progress Chart on page 4.

1 Checkpoint
UNITS 1 AND 2

1 🎧 Listen and follow Ellie's path.

Start → (paper/microscope) → experiment / model / story / poem → desert / river / light / rain →  → Lucky you! / Poor you!

2 Listen to **1** again and answer the questions.

1 What kind of competition did Ellie win?
　_____

2 What did she have to do for the competition?
　_____

3 What kind of experiment did she do?
　_____

4 What did she win?
　_____

3 Read Kiara's email and draw her path in **1**.

Hi Pamela!

Guess what! I entered the Crowford Primary Spring Writing Competition and I wrote a shape poem. I had to create a poem and then write it in a shape. I had to use describing and feeling words. It was difficult but I think I wrote a good poem. It was about a river that passes through many different landscapes like hills, forests, caves and jungles as it travels thousands of kilometres from the mountains to the beach.

The prize was a holiday at a lake. And guess what again! I won! Lucky me!!

Love,
Kiara

4 Put the words in order and write questions.

1. Which / you / win / competition / did / ?
   _____
2. did / you / What / to / do / ? / have
   _____
3. kind of / What / ? / did / you / story / have / to write
   _____
4. did / you / model / have / to make / ? / What / kind of
   _____
5. What / experiment / did / kind of / to do / ? / you / have
   _____
6. ? / poem / did / What / kind of / you / have to / write
   _____
7. did / you / What / win / ?
   _____

5 Ask and answer. Use the questions in 4 and the flowchart in 1.

Which competition did you win?

I won the Science competition.

6 Write a paragraph about one of the topics.

- a competition you won
- a competition you entered
- a poem you wrote
- a story you wrote
- a Science experiment you did

_____
_____
_____
_____
_____

The Outback
CULTURE

1 Read about the Outback again on page 40 of your Pupil's Book. Circle T (True) or F (False).

1	The Australian Outback is on the coast.	T / F
2	There are 10 deserts in the Australian Outback.	T / F
3	There isn't much water in the Australian Outback.	T / F
4	Most Australians live in the Outback.	T / F
5	Most of the people that live in the Outback are farmers.	T / F
6	Some Australian farms are bigger than states in the United States.	T / F

2 Look at the photos and read the article. Circle the best title.

a Jungle Medicine
b Flying Doctors
c Nurses in the Sky

What do you do when you are ill? You probably go to see your local doctor. And if you are very ill, you go to hospital for a few days. But it's completely different if you live in the Australian Outback. There are no doctors there and no hospitals, either. So, what do people do when they are ill? They call the Flying Doctor Service!

The Flying Doctor Service looks after the health of people living in the Outback. Doctors fly in planes long distances to see patients on farms. They bring nurses and medicines with them. It's an excellent service. Flying doctors help people every two minutes on average in the Australian Outback! They have over 60 aeroplanes. In 2017, the planes flew more than 26 million kilometres. That's like 34 trips to the Moon and back!

Sometimes the planes can land on small airstrips near farms, but sometimes there are no airstrips, so they have to land on flat land or motorways. The farmers and their friends light these temporary runways with their car headlights if it's dark. If the ill person needs special treatment or an operation, the plane becomes a flying ambulance. The doctors and nurses put the patient in the plane and fly the patient to the nearest hospital.

3 Complete the sentences.

> car   hospitals   motorways   patients   plane

1. The problem with being ill in the Outback is there aren't any doctors or _____.
2. That is why doctors fly in to see _____.
3. The Flying Doctors' planes need to land on airstrips, _____ or flat land.
4. When there is no proper runway and it is nighttime, people use their _____ headlights to light the runway.
5. When people have to go to hospital, they use the Flying Doctors' _____ as an ambulance.

4 Listen and circle the correct option.

1. Robin Miller was
   a   a doctor.
   b   a nurse.
2. She
   a   could fly a plane.
   b   could not fly a plane.
3. Aboriginal children
   a   had all their vaccinations.
   b   did not have all their vaccinations.
4. Robin Miller flew
   a   flu vaccines to the Outback.
   b   polio vaccines to the Outback.
5. She put the vaccine on
   a   sugar cubes.
   b   biscuits.

5 Think about the last time you were ill and answer the questions.

1. Where did you go?
   _____
2. Who did you see?
   _____
3. How did you get there?
   _____
4. How long did it take to get there?
   _____
5. Have you ever been to hospital?
   _____

I know about the Australian Outback.

3 Hanging out

How can we plan a festival?

1 **Listen and complete the sentences with a word from the box.**

> basketball   bike   helmet
> scooter   skateboards

1. I rode to the park on my _____ yesterday.
2. Two teams were playing _____ on the court in the park.
3. One of our classmates had a brand new _____ with her. She went very fast.
4. We stopped and watched the children use their _____ on the new ramp.
5. Oh, no! That girl didn't have her _____ on. I hope she's OK.

2 **Look and write the sport.**

CODE CRACKER

_____ court

_____ field

_____ court

3 Play *I'm thinking of a word* in groups of four. One person chooses a word from the box in **1**. The others ask questions to guess what it is.

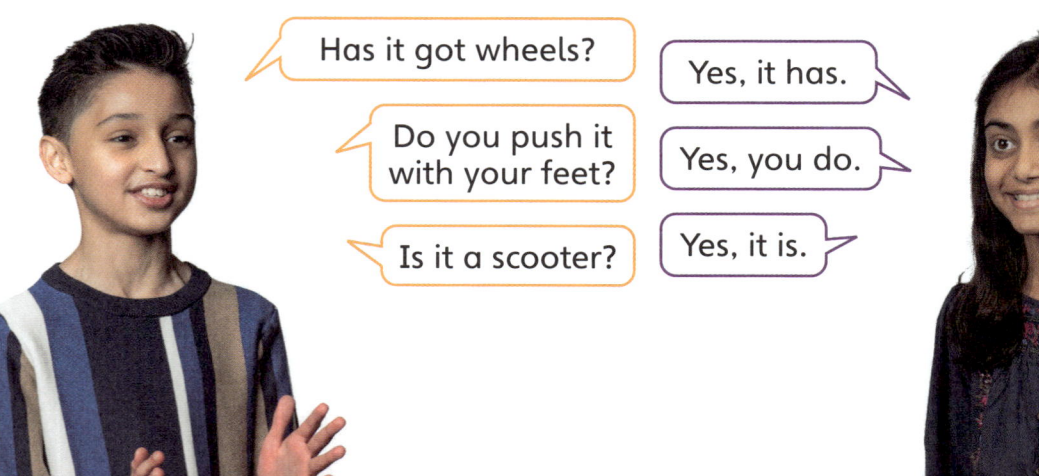

— Has it got wheels?
— Yes, it has.
— Do you push it with your feet?
— Yes, you do.
— Is it a scooter?
— Yes, it is.

A beach festival

VOCABULARY

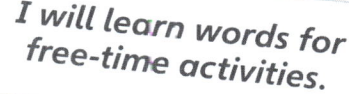
I will learn words for free-time activities.

1 Look and write.

1 _____   2 _____   3 _____

4 _____   5 _____   6 _____

2 Read and complete.

It was Victor's birthday and his uncle Jim gave him a kite, but Victor doesn't like **1** _____ kites. His aunt bought him a **2** _____ to a pop concert to see a famous band, but Victor doesn't like **3** _____ to concerts, either. Victor's dad took him **4** _____ for his birthday and then invited him to a pizza **5** _____ . Victor loves **6** _____ at restaurants.

3  Listen and check your answers to 2.

4 Listen and label the pictures.

elbow pads   helmet   knee pads
riding boots   riding hat   saddle

1 _____
2 _____
3 _____

4 _____
5 _____
6 _____

I can use words for free-time activities.

Language lab

GRAMMAR: FIXED FUTURE PLANS

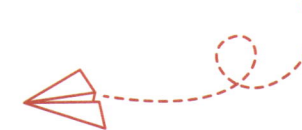

I will talk about fixed plans for the future.

1 Put the words in order and write sentences.

1 festival / ice-skating / tomorrow. / going / We're / an / to
_____

2 ice-skaters / Some / Olympic / doing / are / show. / a
_____

3 too. / We're / skates / our / taking / with us,
_____

4 at / two o'clock / starting / The / show / is / tomorrow afternoon.
_____

5 finishing / It / until / isn't / o'clock / tomorrow. / five
_____

2 Read and complete. Use the verbs in brackets.

OUR PLANS

It's the town festival tomorrow. We're going. Mum and Dad **1** _____ (take) us on the bus. We **2** _____ (meet) all our cousins. There are a lot of things to do there. We **3** _____ (watch) a magic show. Our cousin Jack **4** _____ (enter) the Frisbee competition. I hate throwing Frisbees. We **5** _____ all _____ (have) burgers for lunch, except Lucy. She's a vegetarian. Her mum **6** _____ (make) her cheese sandwiches. Yuck! In the afternoon, I **7** _____ (fly) my new kite, but our cousins **8** _____ (go) home early.

3. Number the sentences in order. Then listen and check.

- [ ] He's meeting his friend David there to prepare the horses.
- [1] Howie is very excited.
- [ ] After riding, they are going to David's house for lunch.
- [ ] He's going to the stables at 10 o'clock.
- [ ] Why? Tomorrow morning he's going horse riding.
- [ ] What an exciting day!
- [ ] And after that they are watching a film together.
- [ ] Then after lunch, they are playing computer games.

4. Look at the diary and write down Chloe's plans.

10:00	go to my dance class
12:00	watch my favourite programme on TV
1:30	have lunch with Grandma and Grandad
3:00	make biscuits with Mum
6:00	play computer games with Harry

Next Saturday at 10 o'clock Chloe's going _____

_____

_____

_____

5. Design a timetable for your Saturday plans.

- Morning ....
- Lunch ....
- Afternoon ....
- Evening

6. Ask and answer with a partner about plans.

What are you doing on Saturday morning?

I'm going horse riding. What about you?

 talk about fixed plans for the future.

Story lab

READING

I will read a story about a birthday.

Hiroki's birthday

1 Read *Hiroki's Birthday* again and circle T (True) or F (False).

1. It was Taro's birthday. T / F
2. Hiroki's mum woke him up in the morning. T / F
3. Hiroki found a note from his grandad in the garden. T / F
4. Hiroki went to play basketball with Taro. T / F
5. Hiroki listened to his favourite band all alone. T / F
6. Everybody forgot Hiroki's birthday. T / F

2 Correct the false statements from **1**.

_____

_____

_____

3 Find words or phrases in the story that mean the same.

1. a bad beginning _____
2. perhaps _____
3. suppose _____
4. the person who serves in a restaurant _____
5. excited about something that's going to happen _____

4 Write the punctuation for direct speech. Check the story on page 48 of your Pupil's Book.

1. ____ Are you going to the skate park today ____ Taro ____ ____ he asked ____
2. Keiko asked ____ ____ Are you looking forward to it ____ ____
3. ____ I can't wait ____ ____ said Hiroki ____ ____ Thank you, everyone ____ ____

5. Complete the conversation for you. Then act it out with your friend.

Your friend: Go on! Open the box!
You: _____
Your friend: Yes! It's for you.
You: _____
Your friend: What is it?
You: _____

6. Write your opinion of the story.

Key
1 = very bad
5 = very good

My opinion
My favourite character is _____ .
My favourite part is _____ .
I think the story is interesting / funny / scary / silly .
I liked / didn't like the story because _____ .
I think it's _____ story. I _____ and
_____ .

① ② ③ ④ ⑤

7. Ask and answer with a partner.

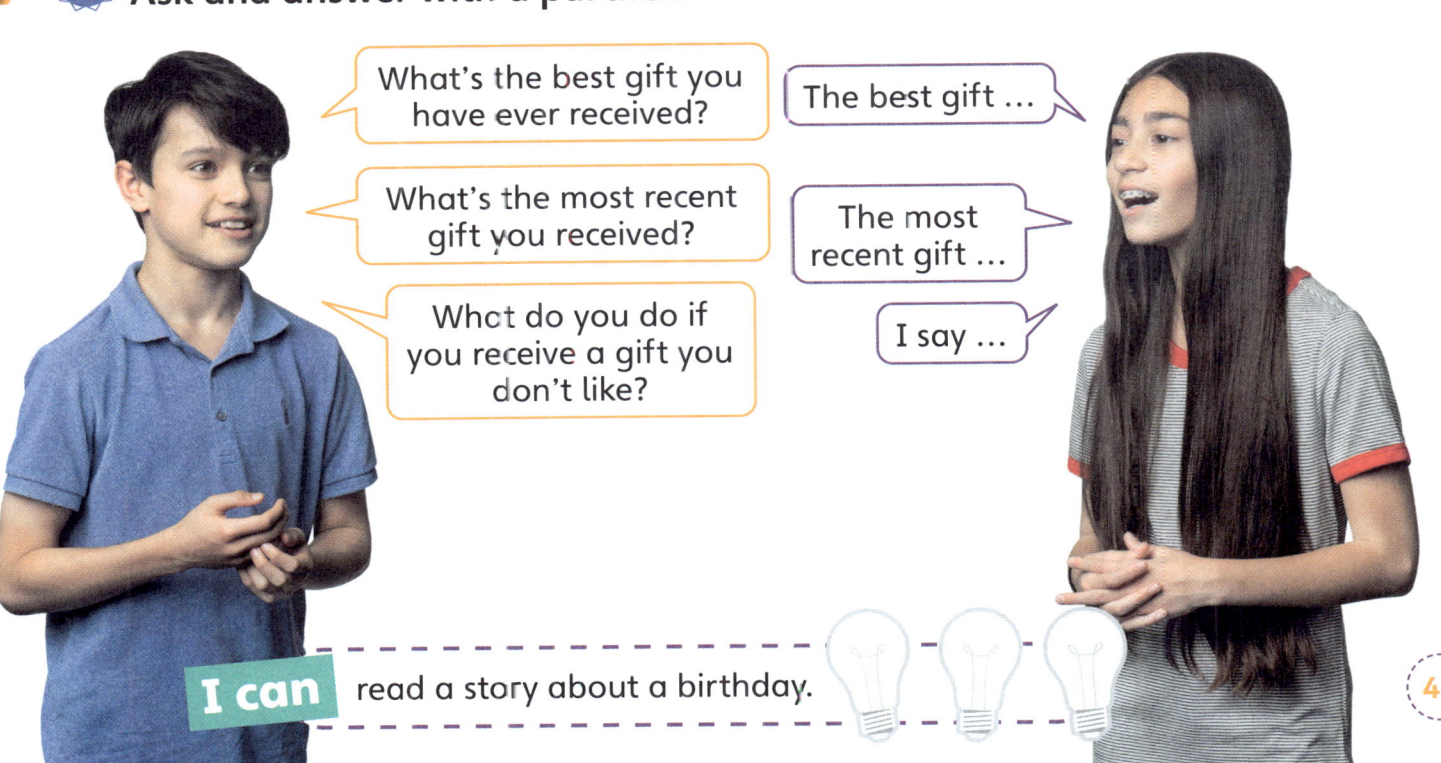

- What's the best gift you have ever received?
- The best gift …
- What's the most recent gift you received?
- The most recent gift …
- What do you do if you receive a gift you don't like?
- I say …

I can read a story about a birthday.

Experiment lab

MATHS: PARTITIONING IN SPORT

I will find out about partitioning and fractions.

1 Look at the shapes and follow the instructions.

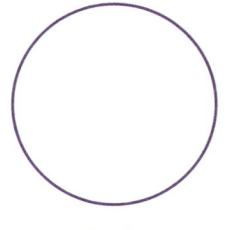
circle
Divide into sixths.

square
Divide in half.

rectangle
Divide into quarters.

2 Read and colour the fractions.

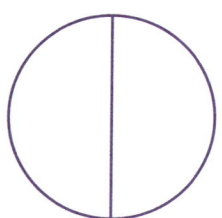 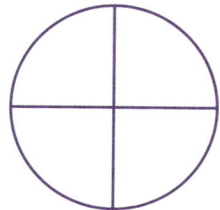  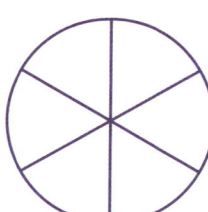 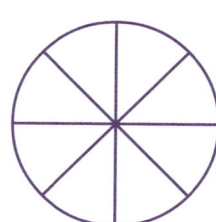

a one-half   b two-fourths   c two-thirds   d five-sixths   e four-eighths   f three-sixths

____   ____   ____   ____   ____   ____

3 Read and write the fractions.

How to write FRACTIONS

Imagine you've got an apple pie. Eight people want a slice, so you are going to cut eight slices. Now imagine you take the first slice from that pie. That slice is one eighth of the apple pie.

When you write a fraction, the top number is the slice you took from the apple pie, the bottom number is the total number of slices.

1/8 is how you write that fraction.

Now think of making slices for different numbers of children. Write the fraction for each.

1 Slices for 3 children: ____
2 Slices for 5 children: ____
3 Slices for 7 children: ____

4 Now write the number fractions under the words in **2**.

EXPERIMENT TIME

Report

1 Look at the information on the football practice card. Write the results in full.

		Number of attempts at goal	Number of goals
1	Derek	4	1
2	Samantha	3	2
3	Fred	5	3
4	Hetty	2	1
5	Mike	8	5

1 Derek scored one quarter of the times he tried.
2 _____
3 _____
4 _____
5 _____

2 Look at the cake, read and solve the maths problems.

MATHS ZONE

Yesterday, Grandma made a cake. She always makes rectangular cakes. She made a rectangular one yesterday, too. She cut the cake into eighths.

She gave one slice to Arabella and another to Grandad. Arabella divided her slice into two halves and shared it with her baby brother. How much of the whole cake did Arabella have?

_____

When it was time to go home, Grandma gave Arabella half of the remaining cake to take home with her. How much of the cake was left for the next day?

_____

3 Reflect on fractions.

Do you find writing fractions easy or difficult? _____

Do you think understanding fractions is a useful skill?
_____

Have you used fractions outside the classroom? _____

I know about partitioning and fractions.

45

When is it happening?

COMMUNICATION: TIME PHRASES

> I will talk about when things are happening.

1 Work in pairs. Ask and answer.

— What time is it?

— It's quarter past two.

2 Look at **1**. Write the times in words.

1 It's _____ .
2 _____
3 _____
4 _____
5 _____
6 _____
7 _____
8 _____

3 Listen and write the times.

Getting up at _____
Swimming class starts at _____
Swimming class ends at _____
Mum picks me up at _____
Hair cut at _____
Back for lunch at _____

4 In pairs, ask and answer about Helen's Saturday morning.

— What's she doing at 11:00?
— She's having her hair cut at 11:00.

5 What are you doing next Saturday?

★ ★ SATURDAY ★ ★
• ....
• ....
• ....
• ....
• ....

6 Ask and answer with your partner. Fill in their plans.

★ ★ SATURDAY ★ ★
• ....
• ....
• ....
• ....
• ....

I can talk about when things are happening.

Writing lab

AN EMAIL ABOUT FUTURE PLANS

I will write an email about future plans.

1 Complete the email with the correct form of the words in brackets.

To: Sophia H Subject: Invitation!

Hi Sophia,

I **1** _____ (go) to a national park next week with some friends from my running team. Do you want to come? This is the plan: We **2** _____ (meet) at school in the morning. We are going by bus.

First, we **3** _____ (eat) lunch together indoors in the canteen. Then we're playing some outdoor games. Next, we **4** _____ (run) around the lake. You love running – you must come! After that, I **5** _____ (play) volleyball on the red team until dinner. Finally, we **6** _____ (watch) a film in the evening. We **7** _____ (not/come) back early. We'll get home around 11 p.m. Is that OK?

Elena

2 Read the email in 1 again and answer the questions.

1 What's Elena doing next week? _____
2 Who is she going with? _____
3 How are they getting there? _____
4 What are they doing there? _____
   _____
5 Are they coming back early? _____

3 Write an email asking a friend to join you at a planned event. Tell them the plan.

_____
_____
_____
_____
_____

I can write an email about future plans.

PROJECT AND REVIEW UNIT 3

Design you own festival

Project report

1 Complete for your festival.

What kind of festival did you design?		What did the plan include?	
☐ book	☐ music	☐ activities	☐ places for activities
☐ street sports	☐ sport	☐ where to eat	☐ bathrooms
☐ dance	☐ _____	☐ entrance	☐ _____
What did your brochure include?		**What did your class think about it?**	
☐ description of events	☐ time of events	☐ They liked it.	☐ They asked questions.
☐ description of food	☐ time for lunch	☐ They made suggestions.	
☐ _____		☐ _____	

2 Complete your project report.

OUR FESTIVAL: _____

What kind of festival did you design?
We designed _____ _____.

What did your brochure include?
It included _____ _____.

What did the plan include?
It included _____ _____.

What did your class think about it?
They _____ _____.

3 Share your report with a partner. Ask questions.

I can design my own festival.

48

Review

1 Complete the phrases. Write go, play or ride.

1 _____ your scooter
2 _____ your skateboard
3 _____ roller-skating
4 _____ baseball
5 _____ horse riding
6 _____ Frisbee
7 _____ volleyball
8 _____ bowling

2 Listen and tick ✓ the correct diary, A or B.

A

Saturday	Sunday
8:00 a.m. get up 9:15 a.m. play volleyball 11:00 a.m. Molly picks me up 1:00 p.m. go bowling	6:00 p.m. homework

B

Saturday	Sunday
8:00 a.m. get up 9:15 a.m. play volleyball 11:00 a.m. Holly picks me up 1:00 p.m. go bowling	8:00 p.m. homework

3 Put the words in order and write sentences.

1 baseball / am playing / at half past five this evening. / I
_____

2 with my mum / I / to the supermarket / am going / between six / and seven o'clock.
_____

3 to school / I / am travelling / by bus today.
_____

4 am going / I / at half past nine. / to bed
_____

4 Complete the sentences for future plans.

1 I _____ (not/play) Frisbee tomorrow.
2 We _____ (play) basketball later today.
3 Who _____ (you/come) to the school concert with this evening?
4 She _____ (go) bowling this afternoon.
5 They _____ (not/watch) TV tonight.

>> Now go to your Progress Chart on page 4.

4 Cinema magic

How can we make a film trailer?

1 Read the descriptions. Write the words.

actor   director   film   scene   script

1   This is the text of a film.   _____
2   This is part of a film or a short piece of action.   _____
3   This is the person on screen who acts in a film.   _____
4   This is something you see at the cinema.   _____
5   This is the person who tells the actors what to do.   _____

2 Complete the information about the film. Use the words from 1.

1   This year's big _____ was about a princess in a glass castle.
2   In one _____ , the princess dramatically rescued the horses.
3   The _____ won an award for making the film.
4   The director said the _____ worked hard and listened to him.
5   The first thing actors do when preparing to act in a film is read the _____ .

3 Listen and check the answers to 2.

4 Number the pictures in order. Then describe them to a partner.

CODE CRACKER

Amazing films

VOCABULARY

I will learn words to talk about films.

1 Read and sort. Use a dictionary to help you.

animation   frightening   interesting   music   scene   sound effects

sight	sound	feelings
_____ _____	_____ _____	_____ _____

2 Read and match.

1 What kind of films do you like?
2 What's your favourite film?
3 What's it about?
4 What's your favourite scene?
5 Who's your favourite actor?

a It's about a magical nanny.
b I like musicals.
c My favourite actor is Emily Blunt.
d I like the scene in the park best.
e It's *Mary Poppins Returns*.

3 In pairs, ask and answer the questions in 2.

4 Listen and label the pictures. What are they watching?

a 3D film   a comedy   a horror film

_____   _____

_____

5 Complete the sentences with **-tion** and **-ph**. Then say.

The dol____in laughed at the anima____ on its ____one.

I can use words to talk about films.

Language lab

GRAMMAR: MAKING COMPARISONS

I will compare things.

1 Read the film reviews and write the titles.

A Dog's Paradise   Miss Kate's Mystery in Texas   Police Patrol   The Finders

My Film Review

1 _____ ★★★★★

This is the year's best film for people who like a good mystery. It's better than the last film set in Mississippi. The special effects are great. There are a lot of explosions because the mystery is set in an oil field. This makes it the most frightening and exciting film in the series.

2 _____ ★★★★☆

This is a clever, interesting and exciting film. It's about two secondary school students and an epidemic at their school that is turning students into zombies. The students use their science skills to find the cure to the zombie disease. The acting, the script and the special effects are amazing.

3 _____ ★★★★☆

This is one of the funniest films I've ever seen. It is full of great jokes and the acting is hilarious. It is about a police officer who loves his patrol car. When someone steals his car, he must go through many crazy and funny experiences to get it back. You'll love it!

4 _____ ★☆☆☆☆

This is the worst film I have ever seen in my life. I love dogs and I usually love any film with a dog in it, but they don't use real dogs. They use computer-generated dogs and it's awful. It isn't funny and I think it's supposed to be a comedy. Don't see it!

2 Read 1 again and answer the questions.

1 Which film is the most frightening?
_____

2 Which film is the funniest?
_____

3 Which film is the worst?
_____

4 Which film is the cleverest?
_____

3 In pairs, write a short song or chant for one of the films in 1.

Two Science kids in a lab,
Doing experiments,
Finding a cure!
Two Science kids in a lab,
Where are they now?

4 Read and circle T (True) or F (False). Then correct the false statements.

What is the most expensive film ever made? Is it *Star Wars: The Rise of Skywalker*? It cost £210 million. Is it *Avengers: Endgame*? It cost £270 million. No one really knows because Hollywood doesn't say. It's a secret.

Which is the most popular film of all time? Is *Star Wars* more popular than *Avengers*? No, 100 million people saw *Avengers* the first weekend. 46 million people saw *Star Wars* the first weekend. Our expert critic said, 'They are both wonderful films. You must see them. *Star Wars* is more frightening than *Avengers* and *Avengers* is funnier than *Star Wars*.'

So, *Avengers* is the biggest film and it's the most expensive, but is it better? What do you think? Which one do you like? Which one is more interesting? Which one is funnier? Which one is more frightening?

1 *Avengers* wasn't as expensive as *Star Wars*.   T / F _____
2 *Avengers* was more popular than *Star Wars*.   T / F _____
3 *Avengers* isn't as funny as *Star Wars*.   T / F _____
4 *Star Wars* isn't as frightening as *Avengers*.   T / F _____

5 Solve the maths problems about the films in 4.

MATHS ZONE

a   What's the difference in revenue?
    270 − 210 = ____ million pounds
b   What's the combined revenue?
    270 + 210 = ____ million pounds
c   What's the total viewing audience?
    100 + 46 = ____ million viewers

6 Think of an actor you like and an actor you don't like. Write their names in the bubbles. Then write sentences to compare them.

A   I like ⟨_____⟩.

B   I don't like ⟨_____⟩.

_____ is better than _____. _____ isn't as interesting as _____.

Values Listen to other people's opinions.

7 In pairs, talk about the actors you chose in 6. Respond to opinions.

I can compare two or more things.

Story lab

READING

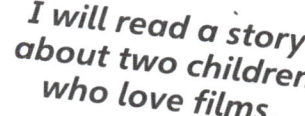

I will read a story about two children who love films.

A LUCKY DAY

1 ⚡ **Match to make phrases from the story *A Lucky Day*.**

1 watch
2 drop something
3 keep
4 turn
5 the most expensive toy

a on the ground
b in the shop
c the money
d a film
e around

2 Read and circle T (True) or F (False).

1 William and Betty's family were rich.   T / F
2 They saw a toy in the shop that cost too much money.   T / F
3 A well-dressed man was early for a film.   T / F
4 He entered the building without realising he dropped something.   T / F

3 ⚡ **Who said it? Write *Betty*, *William* or *Max*.**

1 _____ 'Look, Betty! It goes around and you can see the pictures moving.'
2 _____ 'Yes! But it's the most expensive toy in the shop!'
3 _____ 'I'd love to watch a film.'
4 _____ 'Thank you! The money isn't as important as the papers.'

4 Complete the sentences.

> excited   generous   honest   lucky   poor

1 William and Betty are _____ because they could go to a film.
2 William and Betty are _____ because they gave the man his money and papers.
3 William and Betty are _____ because their family hasn't got a lot of money.
4 William and Betty are _____ because they met a famous director.
5 Max Chapman is _____ because he gave the children the money.

5 Compare yourself to the characters.

I'm not as honest as William and Betty.

I'm as excited about films as William and Betty.

1 _____
2 _____
3 _____
4 _____
5 _____

6 Answer for you. Then ask and answer with a partner.

1 You're looking at a toy. What toy are you looking at?
_____

2 You want to see a film. What film do you want to see?
_____

3 You find some money on the ground. What do you do?
_____

4 Someone gives you a money prize. What do you do with the money?
_____

5 You meet a famous director. What do you say?
_____

7 Think of a film you want to see soon. Read and tick ✓.

1 Do you think the film will be exciting?
I hope so. ☐   I hope not. ☐

2 Do you think there will be any popcorn?
I hope so. ☐   I hope not. ☐

3 Do you think you will like the film?
I hope so. ☐   I hope not. ☐

4 Do you think the tickets will be expensive?
I hope so. ☐   I hope not. ☐

5 Do you think the cinema will be crowded?
I hope so. ☐   I hope not. ☐

6 Do you think your friends will want to see it with you?
I hope so. ☐   I hope not. ☐

I can read a story about two children who love films.

Experiment lab

ART AND DESIGN: HOW DO FILMS WORK?

I will find out how an animation loop works.

1 Read the article *Moving Pictures* again. Then answer in full sentences.

1 What's one image in a film called?
_____

2 How many frames has a film got?
_____

3 How did animators create films in the past?
_____

4 How do animators make animations now?
_____

5 What is a repeated sequence of frames called?
_____

2 Complete the table.

> animation   create   drawing   enjoy   ~~imagination~~   remember   repetition

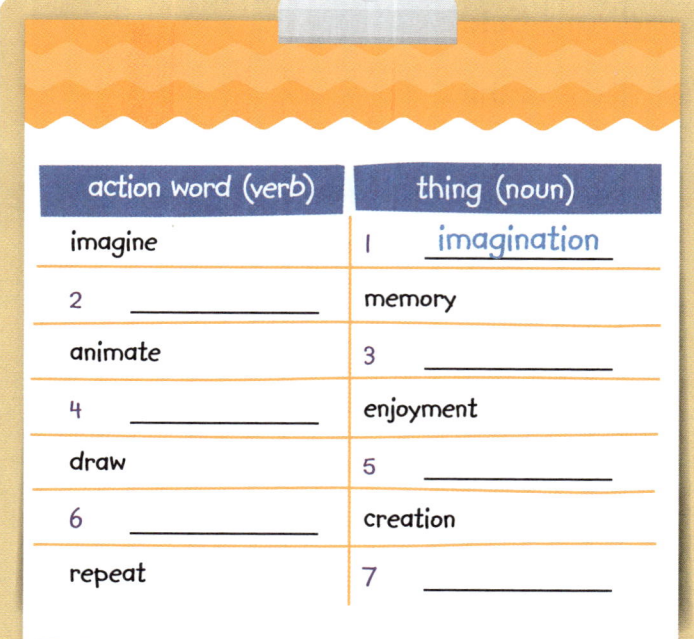

action word (verb)	thing (noun)
imagine	1 imagination
2 _____	memory
animate	3 _____
4 _____	enjoyment
draw	5 _____
6 _____	creation
repeat	7 _____

3 Read and solve the maths problems. Show your work.

MATHS ZONE

1 The film starts at 3:30. It's an hour and a half long. What time does it finish?
_____

2 The actor is 25 years old. The film takes four years to make. How old is the actor at the end of filming?
_____

3 34 million people saw the film *Benjamin Rabbit* the first weekend. 22 million people saw the film *Sandtown* the first weekend. How many more people saw *Benjamin Rabbit* than *Sandtown*?
_____

EXPERIMENT TIME

Report

1 Complete the table. Then share your ideas with a partner.

Things I drew to create an action sequence on a phenakistoscope
A person jumping.

2 Read the example. Then write your own report.

DID THE PHENAKISTOSCOPE WORK?

I drew a person jumping on the paper and attached it to the phenakistoscope. First, I spun it slowly and it didn't work. Then I spun the phenakistoscope quickly, but my eye was too far away from the slit and it didn't work. I had to try about five times to make it work. My biggest problem was getting my eye in the right position to see the image. Finally, I saw the person jumping. Next time, I will draw the pictures more carefully, so the loop looks smoother.

DID THE PHENAKISTOSCOPE WORK?

I drew _____ on the paper and attached it to the phenakistoscope. First, I spun it _____ and _____ . Then I spun the phenakistoscope _____ but _____ .
I had to try about _____ times to make it work. My biggest problem was _____ . Finally, I saw _____ . Next time, I will _____ _____ .

3  Talk about your report with a partner.

I know how an animation loop works.

57

Film-makers

COMMUNICATION: WHAT MIGHT HAPPEN

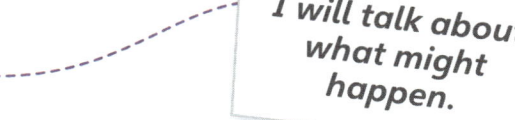
I will talk about what might happen.

1 Unscramble the words and label the pictures.

1. TERWRI

2. UNSOD ENGEERIN

3. ETXARS

4. ADUINECE

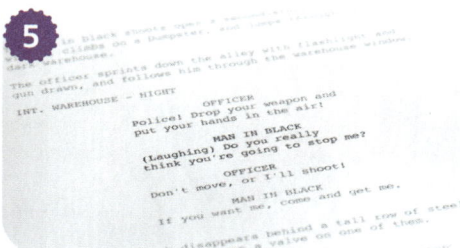
5. ISPCTR

6. TPEORS

2 Read and complete the conversation.

> It might be a musical.   That would be great!   We might see another dance.

Man: They're making a film in the town square.

Woman: Really? What kind of film?

Man: _____
I saw some actors dancing.

Woman: I hope so. Musicals are my favourite films.

Man: Let's go and watch the filming. _____

Woman: Yes, and we might be able to work as extras!

Man: _____

3 Listen and check. Then role-play the conversation.

4 Work in pairs. You are making a film. Say your three biggest worries.

> We might not find any good actors.

> We might have a terrible director.

I can talk about what might happen.

Writing lab

A FILM REVIEW

I will write a film review.

1 Write the names of three films you have seen recently and colour the stars.

Film title	Rating
1	☆ ☆ ☆ ☆ ☆
2	☆ ☆ ☆ ☆ ☆
3	☆ ☆ ☆ ☆ ☆

2 Choose one film from **1** and write what happens.

_____
_____
_____
_____

3 Make a poster for the film you wrote about in **2**. Include the following:

Live action or animation?	
Number of actors	
Names of two main characters	
Who will or might enjoy it?	

4 Read the example. Then write a review of the film.

- What's it about?
- What's your opinion of the film?
- Why did you like it?
- Who would like it?

> I recently saw *The Dragomads*. It was great and I recommend it to anyone who likes animated films about animals. It's about a group of homeless dragons who travel the world looking for the best place to live. I liked it because the story was original and exciting. I think it's a good film for anyone from 8 to 12 years old. I give it four stars.

_____
_____
_____
_____

I can write a film review.

PROJECT AND REVIEW — UNIT 4

Make a film trailer

Project report

1 Think about your film trailer and answer the questions.

What kinds of trailers did you watch for research?	What film did you choose to make a trailer for?
_____ _____ _____ _____	_____
	Which three scenes did you choose?
	_____ _____
Who took these roles? director: _____ camera operator: _____ actors: _____ voice-over: _____ sound effects: _____ music: _____	**What part of your trailer was difficult to make?** _____ _____
	Did you need to make changes to your storyboard or script? _____ _____
	What feedback did you get about your trailer? _____

2 Write your project report using the answers in **1**.

Project report – Make a film trailer
_____
_____
_____
_____
_____

3 Share your report with a partner. Ask questions.

 **I can** make a film trailer.

Review

1 Circle words in the word snake.

famous sceneactor director film frightening sound effects script animation expensive character science fiction

2 Complete with words from the word snake.

Steven Spielberg is a very famous **1** _____ . His **2** _____ include *E.T. The Extra-Terrestrial* (1982) and *Jurassic Park* (1993). These are **3** _____ _____ films. *Jurassic Park* is about an imagined natural world and *E.T.* is about an alien stuck on Earth. *Jurassic Park* is scarier than *E.T.* *E.T.* is one of Spielberg's most loved characters. He doesn't talk much, but he's got one of the most **4** _____ lines in film history, 'E.T. phone home.' The **5** _____ where he says that line is filmed in Elliot's sister's bedroom. If you want to read the **6** _____ for *E.T.*, you can find it on the internet. The actors in *E.T.* were children. The **7** _____ of Elliot was 10 years old. Henry Thomas played Elliot, and Elliot's sister, Gertie, was played by Drew Barrymore, who is now one of the most famous **8** _____ in Hollywood.

3 Complete the table.

funnier	the funniest
better	1 _____
2 _____	the worst
3 _____	the most interesting
more famous	4 _____
more frightening	5 _____
6 _____	the most exciting

4 Read and circle the correct words.

Boy: It **1** might / might not rain. Let's go to the cinema and not the park.

Girl: The film **2** might / might not have good sound effects. It's about extra-terrestrials on Earth.

Boy: I don't know. It **3** might / might not be interesting. Alan said it was boring.

Girl: Hmm. What else can we see? Oh, this film **4** might / might not be good. It's about a lost dog that travels thousands of kilometres to get home.

Boy: It **5** might / might not be sad. You'd better take a tissue.

Girl: Wait. I **6** might / might not have enough money.

>> Now go to your Progress Chart on page 4.

2 Checkpoint
UNITS 3 AND 4

1 🎧 027 **Listen and follow Ben's path.**

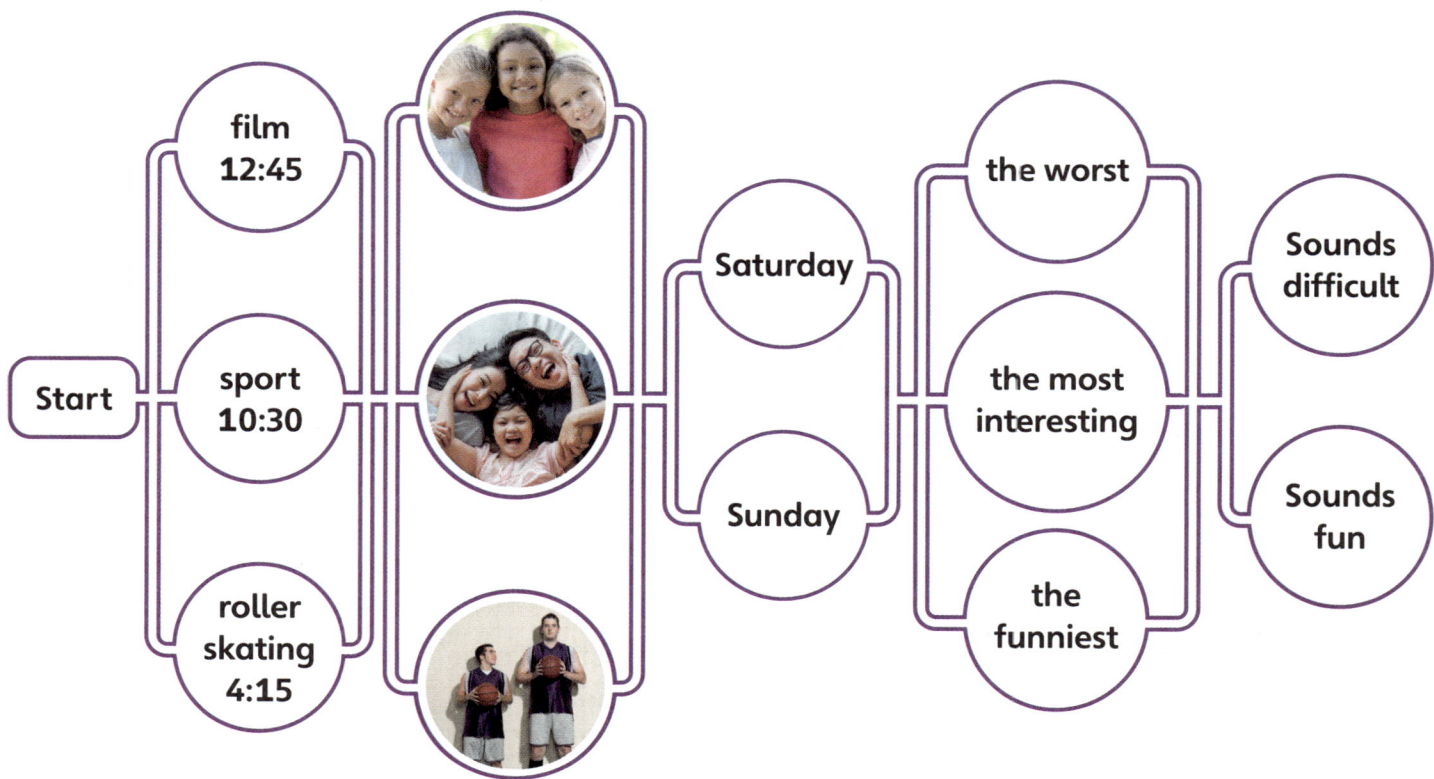

2 Look at and listen to 1 again. Circle the best answer.

1 Who is Ben playing basketball with on Saturday morning?
   a his family
   b his teammates
2 Does Ben like windy weather?
   a Yes, he does.
   b No, he doesn't.
3 What's he doing on Sunday?
   a He's doing a fun project.
   b He's doing a boring project.
4 What kind of films are the worst according to the girl?
   a animation
   b horror

3 🎧 028 **Listen and follow Kelly's path in 1.**

4 Read the review of the film Kelly saw and answer the questions.

⭐⭐⭐⭐⭐ *Lucas at Work* is a fantastic live action comedy film.

By Kelly Smith – 18 July

It's the funniest film this year! The main character is called Lucas Delucia. The actor who plays him is Cameron Buttersworth. He's my favourite actor because I think he's really good at doing funny scenes.

At the beginning of the film, Lucas meets a group of neighbourhood kids who want to solve an old town mystery. They are all bored because they've got nothing to do over the summer. All the characters in the film are very silly and very funny. I love the film because a lot of interesting and crazy things happen. The special effects are amazing, too. The best part is when the mayor is chasing them down the street on a scooter.

I think children, teenagers and adults will love this film.

1. What is the film called? _____
2. What kind of film is it? _____
3. Does Kelly like the film? How do you know? _____
4. What words describe the characters? _____
5. Who would enjoy the film? _____

5  Write a review of a film you've seen.

> animation   characters   director   exciting   funny   interesting
> live action   scary   science fiction   sound effects   special effects

_____
_____
_____
_____

6 Talk about what you're doing on Saturday and Sunday with a partner.

What are you doing on Saturday?

I'm playing football with my teammates.

Sakura
CULTURE

1 🎧 029 **Listen to the conversation and answer the questions.**

1 What are the children talking about?
   _____

2 What was the girl crazy about before?
   _____

3 What does she like now?
   _____

4 What does the boy like about his choice?
   _____

2 Read and answer the questions.

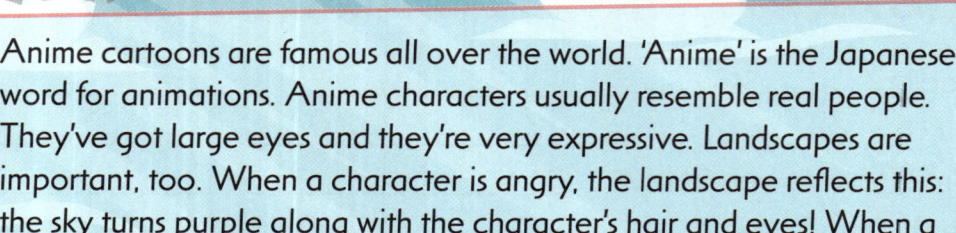

Anime cartoons are famous all over the world. 'Anime' is the Japanese word for animations. Anime characters usually resemble real people. They've got large eyes and they're very expressive. Landscapes are important, too. When a character is angry, the landscape reflects this: the sky turns purple along with the character's hair and eyes! When a character is happy, the sky is bright and clear.

To make anime, Japanese artists create hand-drawn pictures in black and white. Each picture is called a frame. The artists put the frames together. Then the pictures are put onto a computer and digitally coloured.

To draw 60 to 90 seconds of cartoon takes an anime artist about six weeks. We can often see anime episodes on TV. Each episode lasts 24 minutes and needs 34,560 frames! So next time you see an anime clip, think of all the hard work behind it.

1 Where does 'anime' come from?
   Anime comes from _____ .
2 What do anime characters usually look like?
   Anime characters _____ .
3 Why is colour so important in Anime cartoons?
   Colour _____ .
4 What is special about the way the artists create the drawings?
   The artists _____ .

64

3 Interview six people to find out which TV cartoons they like best.

Name	Favourite cartoon	What do you like about it?
1		
2		
3		
4		
5		
6		

4 Write about a popular cartoon in your country. What is it about? Who are the central characters? Where do they live? What do they do?

5 In groups, invent a cartoon character. Think about what is special about the character. Draw a picture of your cartoon character. Look at the Ideas Box below.

Can your character fly?
Is it strong?
Is it an animal?
Where does it live?
What does it do?

6 In the same groups, write a short story with your ideas from **5**.

I know about Sakura and Japanese anime.

5 Once in a lifetime

How can we plan the trip of a lifetime?

1 Label the pictures.

helicopter   lake   mountain   pilot   train   underground

1 _____
2 _____
3 _____
4 _____
5 _____
6 _____

2 Unscramble the words and complete.

I live in the city. I travel to school by
1 _____ (RDRONEUGUDN). There are
2 _____ (NDWIOSW), but there is no
3 _____ (VWEI) because you are in a tunnel. All you can see are black walls. It's very 4 _____ (NISOY). It makes a loud sound that hurts my ears, but I don't mind because it's fast. I think it is the best way to 5 _____ (TERAVL) when you are in a city.

3 Listen and check the answers to 2.

4 Complete using the code.

CODE CRACKER

!	&	%	£	@	#	>	}
b	f	n	a	o	c	k	p

1 Be careful when you get @% and @&& the train in the underground.
_____ _____

2 Don't wear your !£#>}£#>.
Take it @&& and carry it.
_____ _____

Let's explore!

VOCABULARY

I will learn words to talk about travel experiences.

1 Read and sort.

climb up a tower   feed the penguins   fly in a helicopter   fly in a hot-air balloon
go camping   go snorkelling   go up a mountain   ride a camel
see a hummingbird   stay in a hotel   visit a palace

on land	in the sea	in the air	with animals
_____	_____	_____	_____
_____	_____	_____	_____
_____	_____	_____	_____

2 Read the clues and circle the activity.

1 The air is fresh. There are trees and there's a dirt path. My legs are tired.
   a I'm travelling by underground.
   b I'm flying in a hot-air balloon.
   c I'm hiking up a mountain.

2 We go up suddenly. Now we move forwards. We're in the air. It's very noisy.
   a We're climbing up a tower.
   b We're flying in a helicopter.
   c We're snorkelling.

3 Ask and answer with a partner.

1 Would you like to stay in a hotel or go camping?
2 Would you prefer to ride a camel or feed the penguins?
3 Would you like to visit a palace or see a hummingbird?
4 Would you rather go snorkelling or fly in a hot-air balloon?

4 Ph 031 Write the words in the table based on the end sounds /s/, /z/ or /iz/. Then listen, check and repeat.

backpacks   boxes   buses   camels
cars   donkeys   mountains   palaces
suitcases   tents

/s/	/z/	/iz/
_____	_____	_____
_____	_____	_____
_____	_____	_____
_____	_____	_____

I can use words to talk about travel experiences.

Language lab

GRAMMAR: TALKING ABOUT LIFE EXPERIENCES

I will talk about experiences I've had in my life.

1 Write the correct form of the verbs in brackets.

Have you ever …
1 _____ (climb) a climbing wall at a gym?
2 _____ (hike) in a national park?
3 _____ (stay) in a cabin?
4 _____ (fly) in a plane?
5 _____ (ride) horse?
6 _____ (see) a horror film?
7 _____ (feed) the ducks in the park?

2 Ask and answer the questions in **1**.

Have you ever climbed a climbing wall at a gym?

Yes, I have. / No, I haven't.

3 Read and complete the things that Lilian has and hasn't done.

Lilian loves going on holiday. She's been hiking a lot of times, but she's never **1** _____ (climb up) a tower and she's never **2** _____ (visit) a palace. She's never **3** _____ (go) camping, either. But next summer, she and her family are going to go to Ireland to do all of that!

In Ireland, they will travel by car and by train. Lilian has travelled by car, bus and taxi but she's never **4** _____ (travel) by train.

They will visit the Dublin Zoo to feed the penguins. Lilian has never **5** _____ (feed) penguins before, but she has **6** _____ (ride) a camel and she has **7** _____ (see) a hummingbird.

4 Look at the table and complete the questions and answers.

Tell us about your experiences.	Kim	Karen	Helena	Andrew	Morris
hike up a mountain	no	yes	no	yes	yes
travel by boat	no	no	no	yes	no
visit a palace	yes	yes	yes	yes	no
ride a camel	no	no	yes	yes	no
see a hummingbird	yes	yes	yes	no	yes
fly in a helicopter	no	yes	no	no	yes
feed a deer	yes	no	no	no	yes
stay in a tent	no	yes	no	yes	yes

1 ____Has____ Karen ____hiked____ up a mountain? ____Yes, she has.____
2 _____ Andrew _____ by boat? _____
3 _____ Helena and Andrew _____ a palace? _____
4 _____ Kim ever _____ a camel? _____
5 _____ Helena and Morris _____ a hummingbird? _____
6 _____ Andrew ever _____ in a helicopter? _____
7 _____ Kim and Morris _____ a deer? _____
8 _____ Kim _____ in a tent? _____
9 _____ Andrew and Morris _____ in a tent? _____

5 Talk about what the people in 4 have and haven't done.

> Has Helena ever stayed in a tent?
> No, she hasn't.

6 Write three things from this lesson you've done and three things you've never done.

I've _____ .   I've never _____ .
I've _____ .   I've never _____ .
I've _____ .   I've never _____ .

7 Tell your partner about your lists in 6.

> I've stayed in a tent.
> I've never fed a deer.

I can talk about experiences I've had in my life.

Story lab

READING

> I will read a fable about two travellers.

The travellers and the bear, by Aesop

1 Read *The travellers and the bear* again. Then number the events in order.

a   The man lay down on the ground.   ☐
b   The woman asked him what the bear had said.   ☐
c   Two travellers were on a journey around the world.   1
d   They heard a terrible roar.   ☐
e   The bear whispered to the man.   ☐
f   The woman ran to a tree and climbed up it.   ☐

2 Complete with *woman*, *man* or *bear*.

A 1 _____ and a 2 _____ were hiking through a forest. Suddenly, they heard a terrible roar and screamed. The 3 _____ ran to a tree and climbed up. The 4 _____ remembered an interesting fact. The 5 _____ could feel the 6 _____'s sharp claws and soft fur. The 7 _____'s heart was beating fast. After a moment, the 8 _____ walked away. 'Was the 9 _____ talking to you?' the 10 _____ asked. And the 11 _____ walked on, a wiser man.

3 Read and solve the maths problems.

MATHS ZONE

1   A brown bear eats 35 kilograms of food a day. How much food does it eat in five days? _____

2   A brown bear weighs 310 kilograms before hibernation. It weighs half that after hibernation. How much does it weigh after hibernation? _____

3   A brown bear enters its den at the end of October and stays for six months. When does it come out? _____

4 Read the title of Aesop's fable and circle what you think the fable is about. Then skim the story and check.

THE DOG AND THE BONE

I think it's about …

a a crow that likes to sing.   b a clever fox.   c a greedy dog.   d a race.

5 Read the fable and write the moral.

One day, a butcher gave a hungry dog a nice meaty bone. The dog was very happy as it walked away carrying the bone in its mouth. The dog walked a short distance until it reached a bridge. It stopped at the centre of the bridge and started its feast. Suddenly, it looked down into the water and saw another dog with a bone in its mouth. This other dog was looking up with angry eyes. The greedy dog thought, 'I want my bone and that bone, too.' The dog opened its mouth to bark at the dog in the water. As soon as the dog opened its mouth, the bone fell with a splash into the stream. The dog jumped into the stream, but of course, there was no dog in the water and no bone, either. In fact, the dog now had no bone. Its bone was at the bottom of the stream and the other bone was nothing but a reflection!

The moral of the fable is _____ _____ .

6 Create a cartoon based on the fable *The Dog and the Bone*.

I can read a fable about two travellers.

Experiment lab

SCIENCE: ANIMALS AROUND THE WORLD

I will find out about the different features of animals.

1 Read the definitions and write the words.

1. the hard pointed mouth of a bird _____
2. a sharp curved nail on some animals' feet _____
3. a large round shape that rises above the surface of something _____
4. the part of a bird's or insect's body that it uses for flying _____
5. the thick, soft hair that covers the bodies of some animals _____

2 Do the quiz. Circle a or b.

Animal Quiz!

1 A porcupine has got sharp needles on its body to
  a protect it from predators.
  b look attractive in the forest.

2 A porcupine's long claws help it
  a run fast when in danger.
  b find food in forests and deserts.

3 Thick hair on a camel's body keeps it
  a colourful and bright.
  b warm or cool.

4 Big, flat feet help a camel walk on
  a sand.
  b water.

5 Fat in the camel's humps provides ____ when there isn't any food.
  a water
  b energy

6 Hummingbirds live in
  a Western and Eastern Europe.
  b North and South America.

7 Hummingbirds are the ____ birds in the world.
  a smallest
  b biggest

8 Hummingbirds' wings move very fast, so they
  a travel long distances and glide on the wind.
  b stay in the same place for a long time.

3 Read, look and match.

1. The pelican's beak expands to become a big spoon for collecting food. They eat fish.

2. The robin's beak is long and thin. It's shaped for digging in the ground and picking up worms.

3. Eagles' beaks are curved and strong. They eat small mammals like rabbits and they also eat fish.

4. Cardinals have got short triangular beaks which are strong enough to break the hard shells of nuts and seeds.

EXPERIMENT TIME

Report

1 Write the tools you used as beaks. Use a dictionary if needed.

Tools we used as beaks	Tools that weren't useful
_____ _____ _____	_____ _____ _____

2 Tell your partner the tools that worked the best for the food you chose.

3 Write your report.

The best tools to use as beaks

I know about the different features of animals.

73

At the tourist office

COMMUNICATION: ASKING FOR INFORMATION

I will ask for information.

1 Complete the conversation.

A: Excuse me, where can we see penguins?

B: You _____ do that at the beach. There's a bus tour from here.

A: Can we feed the penguins?

B: No, you _____ . It's not allowed. But you can watch the penguin parade. It's amazing.

A: How long does it take?

B: The tour is four hours _____ . The bus trip is an hour each way, and the penguin parade is two _____ long.

A: How much does it cost?

B: It's £35 for an adult and £15 for a _____ .

A: Great! I'd _____ two tickets, please.

B: Here you are. £50, please.

A: _____ you.

2 Listen and check the answers to **1**.

3 Read and complete. Then ask and answer about the tours.

Activity: See a koala
Where: Koala Park in the mountains near Sydney, Australia
Length of trip: ½ hour by bus from city, 3 hours to visit the park
Cost: Park entrance = £15
Bus ride = £7 per person

Activity: Feed the dolphins
Where: _____
_____
Length of trip: _____
_____
Cost: _____

4 In pairs, role-play buying tickets for the activities in **3**.

- Three return tickets to the Koala Park, please.
- That's £21, please.
- Here you are.
- Thank you.

I can ask for information.

Writing lab

WRITING AN INTERVIEW

I will write an article about an interview.

1 Read the interview. Write the questions and match the photos.

Have you ever been to the desert?   Where are you now?   Why do you enjoy travelling?

Q: _____

A: Yes, I have. I went to the desert last year. It's the most amazing place in the world! I climbed a big sand dune. It was like a mountain of sand. It took six hours to travel across the desert from the road to the sand dune by camel.   Photo _____

Q: _____

A: I'm in the middle of the amazing country of Turkey! I'm travelling by bus to the town of Cappadocia from the capital city, Ankara. The hot-air balloons of Cappadocia fly every day at sunrise. It's beautiful! I want to take pictures from the air.   Photo _____

Q: _____

A: I enjoy travelling because I like visiting new places and I like meeting interesting people. I like taking photographs of amazing things.   Photo _____

2 Write another paragraph for the interview above.

Where would you like to go next?

I'd like to go _____.

I've never _____.

3 Make some flag bunting with countries you have visited or want to visit.

I can write an article about an interview.

PROJECT AND REVIEW — UNIT 5

Plan the trip of a lifetime

Project report

1 Complete for your group.

Things you have never done but would like to do	A country you would like to go to
_____ _____	_____ _____
Amazing experiences you can have there	**Places you marked on your chosen country's map**
_____ _____	_____ _____
Ways you will travel	**Information about each trip**
_____ _____	_____ _____

2 Complete your project report.

Our trip of a lifetime

Our group will go to the United States. We will start in Los Angeles. We will go to Disneyland in Anaheim. It takes about 50 minutes by bus from the airport to the park and costs £35 each. We have never been to California. From there, we will go to the San Diego Zoo ...

Our trip of a lifetime

3 Create a short video about your trip of a lifetime.

This is our trip of a lifetime.

I can plan the trip of a lifetime.

Review

1 Unscramble and write the travel experiences.

1 RDIE A CAEML _____
2 FYL NI A HTO-IAR BLAOLON _____
3 OG MAGPCNI _____
4 HIEK PU A MONUATIN _____

2 Match to make questions.

1 How long
2 How much
3 Where can we
4 Have you ever
5 What would you like

a held a snake?
b go and see the pandas?
c does the tour take?
d to do next?
e does the ticket cost?

3 Complete the questions and answers.

1 Q: _____ you _____ a camel?
A: Yes, I _____ .

2 Q: _____ you ever _____ snorkelling?
A: No, I _____ .

3 Q: _____ she _____ in a helicopter?
A: No, she _____ .

4 Q: _____ they ever _____ in a hotel?
A: Yes, they _____ .

5 Q: _____ we _____ camping?
A: Yes, we _____ .

4 Ask and answer.

- Have you ever seen a hummingbird?
- Have you gone snorkelling?
- Do you prefer travelling by underground or by car?
- Where would you like to go?
- How much does a tour in your city or town cost?
- What would you like to do?

Now go to your Progress Chart on page 4.

6 Codes and clues

How and why do we use codes?

1 Read the clues and write the words.

1. A mark made on the ground while walking in snow or mud. _____
2. Something dark you wear over your eyes to protect them from bright light. _____
3. You need one to tell the time. You usually wear it on your arm. _____
4. It's sweet and very cold. It sometimes comes in a cone. _____
5. You can listen to music with these, but no one else can hear it. _____
6. Birds can make their nests in it. You can sit in its shade. _____

2 Match the words in **1** to the pictures.

3 Solve the code and write the message.

CODE CRACKER

Mfu't hp po b usfbtvsf ivou.

Let's ____ ____ ___ _____ _____ .

78

Clues

VOCABULARY

I will learn words for possessions.

1 Look and write.

  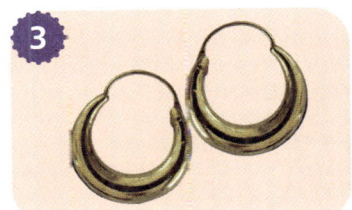 

1 _____   2 _____   3 _____   4 _____

2 Answer the riddles.

1. I've got numbers on my face. You wear me. What am I? _____
2. People use me to keep their trousers up. What am I? _____
3. People make me with their fingers on surfaces. What am I? _____
4. We are worn as decoration on ears. What are we? _____
5. I take other people's things and sometimes go to prison. What am I? _____
6. I am round and people wear me on their fingers. What am I? _____

3 Write a riddle with a partner. Share your riddle with the class.

_____

4 Read the sentences. Circle the correct ending sounds of the underlined words. Listen, check and say.

1. A thief <u>walked</u> into the museum.   /t/   /d/
2. He <u>looked</u> at the ring on display.   /t/   /d/
3. He <u>opened</u> the case.   /t/   /d/
4. He <u>reached</u> for the ring.   /t/   /d/
5. But the museum guard <u>rushed</u> into the room.   /t/   /d/
6. He <u>knocked</u> down the thief.   /t/   /d/
7. He <u>called</u> the police.   /t/   /d/
8. They <u>followed</u> the thief.   /t/   /d/

I can use words for possessions.

Language lab

GRAMMAR: SHORT/LONG EVENTS IN THE PAST

I will talk about two events happening in the past.

1 Complete the story with the correct form of the words in brackets.

I was playing in the park when I **1** _____ (hear) a dog bark. When I looked around, a man **2** _____ (put) a rope around the dog's neck. He **3** _____ (pull) the dog along the path when a woman shouted 'Stop! That's my dog!' She **4** _____ (trip) and fell when she was running after the man. I **5** _____ (run) after the thief when the dog escaped. It ran back to its owner.

2 Read the story and complete the questions.

The children were changing their clothes after swimming class when Celia screamed. Everyone stopped and looked around. 'Who stole my new trainers?' shouted Celia. She was crying. The teacher was just coming into the changing room. She saw Celia crying and heard what she said. 'OK, everyone. Stop what you're doing and look for Celia's shoes.' Everyone started to look for the trainers. The teacher was watching everybody when Trisha found the trainers under a bench. Celia looked embarrassed. All the other girls were feeling angry.

'You see, Celia?' said the teacher. 'No one stole your shoes. You didn't put them away! Apologise right now.'

'I'm sorry', said Celia.

came doing found told
were what when when

1 What _____ the children doing _____ Celia screamed?

2 _____ was Celia doing when the teacher _____ into the changing room?

3 What was the teacher _____ when Trisha _____ the trainers?

4 How were the other girls feeling _____ the teacher _____ Celia to apologise?

3 Work in pairs. Ask and answer the questions in 2.

80

4 What were the children doing when the break bell rang? Look and write.

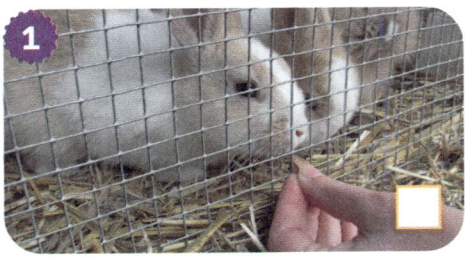
Amy / feed / rabbits
Amy was feeding the rabbits when the break bell rang.

Jack / climb / tree
_____

Dan and Henry / play / football
_____

They / skip
_____

Suzie / eat / pizza
_____

Ellie / read / book
_____

5 Look at the pictures in 4 again. Listen to the questions and circle the correct answers.

1 Yes, she was. / No, she wasn't.
2 Yes, he was. / No, he wasn't.
3 Yes, they were. / No, they weren't.
4 Yes, they were. / No, they weren't.
5 Yes, she was. / No, she wasn't.
6 Yes, she was. / No, she wasn't.

6 Write questions about yesterday.

1 What / teacher / do / you / arrive / class
   What _____?

2 What / you / do / friend / arrive / school
   What _____?

3 What / you / do / bell / ring / for class
   What _____?

I can talk about two events happening in the past.

Story lab

READING

> I will read a story about a secret message.

A Secret Message

1 Read *A Secret Message* again. Number the events in the correct order.

a   Harriet was writing out the sentences when the others went to the Viking museum. ☐
b   She didn't hear the question so she couldn't answer it. ☐
c   Harriet was dreaming when Miss Brown asked her a question. ☐ 1
d   She told her to write 'I must listen to my teacher' 100 times. ☐
e   Harriet discovered a secret message on the paper. ☐
f   The security guard and Harriet found that the belt was missing. ☐
g   A thief was going to steal a gold belt from the museum! ☐
h   Miss Brown was wearing the gold belt! ☐
i   Harriet ran to the museum fast. ☐
j   They followed a piece of green wool to Miss Brown. ☐

2 Answer the questions about the story.

1   What did Harriet find when she was writing the sentences for Miss Brown?
_____

2   What was missing in the exhibition?
_____

3   How did the security guard and Harriet know that Miss Brown was the thief?
_____

3 Read and solve the maths problems.

MATHS ZONE

Harriet had to write 100 lines but she only wrote three quarters of her lines. How many lines did she write?

The museum was 1 mile from the school and Harriet ran at 6 miles per hour. How long did it take her to get to the museum?

4 Find words or phrases in *A Secret Message* that mean:

1. a school outing _____
2. not having a smooth surface _____
3. hidden information in writing _____
4. perhaps _____
5. work out the clues _____
6. jewellery you wear on your wrist _____

5 Work in pairs. Discuss the questions.

1. Can you describe Harriet's behaviour at the beginning of the story?
2. What was Miss Brown's behaviour like?
3. Was Harriet's punishment fair or unfair?
4. Was she right to go to the museum alone?

6 Read the instructions. Make invisible ink.

WRITING SECRET MESSAGES IS FUN!

Pretend to be a secret agent and write a secret message to other secret agents! You can write it in invisible ink.

| Squeeze half a lemon into a cup. | Add a few drops of water and mix. | Write your message with a cotton bud on white paper. |

Let your secret message dry. How can another secret agent read your message? The secret agent holds the message close to a lamp and waits. Look! The message appears!

7 Where's the thief? Write a message to another secret agent using invisible ink. Can the other agent read your message? Write the message you received.

_____

I can read a story about a secret message.

Experiment lab
ENGINEERING AND TECHNOLOGY: CIPHERS

I will find out about the history of codes and ciphers.

1 Read *Codes and Ciphers* on page 96 of your Pupil's Book again. Then match to make sentences.

1 Mary Queen of Scots
2 Julius Caesar used D
3 There are only two written symbols
4 The first emails
5 People encrypt information

a used binary code.
b wrote secret messages in prison.
c in secret codes.
d instead of A in his cipher.
e in a binary code.

2 Read the text below and circle T (True) or F (False).

1 George Washington spied against the British.   T / F
2 His secret agent name was 007.   T / F
3 He needed to communicate with his soldiers.   T / F
4 He wrote messages to his soldiers in code.   T / F
5 Washington invented invisible ink on his own.   T / F
6 The British won the War of Independence.   T / F

One of the most famous spies in American history was George Washington. He was a political leader and a military general. When he was a secret agent, his secret agent name was 711. He was head of a very successful group of spies who collected information on the movement of enemy soldiers. He led the American forces in their War of Independence against the British. He later became the first President of the United States. During the revolution, he had to send messages to his soldiers. He didn't want the enemy to read and understand the messages, so he wrote them in cipher. His secret messages helped the United States defeat the British army. To keep the messages extra secret, Washington helped a man called James Jay to create an invisible ink. This was the first invisible ink in history.

3 Answer the questions.

1 What did Washington's spy group do?
_____

2 Why did Washington write messages in code?
_____

3 Who did he write them to?
_____

4 What was Washington called when he was a secret agent?
_____

5 What did Washington help James Jay do?
_____

EXPERIMENT TIME

Report

1 Write the steps you took to create your cipher.

_____
_____
_____
_____

2 Write a report about your experiment. Did the experiment work? Why? Why not?

My experiment worked/didn't work because _____.

One thing that worked well was _____.

One thing that didn't work well was _____.

I learnt to _____.

I enjoyed/didn't enjoy it because _____ _____.

I know about the history of codes and ciphers.

Are you sure?

COMMUNICATION: HOW CERTAIN YOU ARE

I will express how certain I am.

1 Work in pairs. Read the clues and talk about who you think has got Jonathan's skateboard now. How certain are you? Who stole Jonathan's skateboard?

Jonathan is in the park. His skateboard has disappeared. There were only four other people in the park at the time …

Davey is a friend of Jonathan's. He loves skateboarding, but he hasn't got a skateboard. He lost his board a month ago.

Samantha was playing in the park for 15 minutes and then went home. Nobody knows Samantha.

Peter is only six. He's very good at roller skating. He wants to have a skateboard, but his mum thinks they're dangerous.

All the children know the ice cream lady. She's very popular in the park. She's got a son of her own. He'll be 11 next week.

I think … What about you?

It could be … because …

Are you sure?

It might be …

It must be …

Yes, I'm certain.

2 Write your conclusions. Share them with the class.

I can express how certain I am.

Writing lab

WRITING A DIARY

I will write a diary entry.

1 Share a code you have created with a partner. Then write your partner's code.

2 Write about a time you lost something or something was stolen from you.

> One day I was walking home from school when I dropped some money. I didn't notice …

3 Use the secret code you learnt in **1** to write one more line about how you felt in **2**.

4 Swap diaries with your partner. Can you decode your partner's code in **3**?

I can write a diary entry.

Create a treasure hunt

Project report

1 Review the treasure hunt. Complete the table.

Which hidden items did you find?	Which codes were difficult to crack?
We found _____ _____ _____ _____ _____ _____	The first code was _____.
	There was a _____.
	Which codes were easy to crack?
	It was easy to crack _____.
	The easiest _____.
	Write an example of a code you read. _____ _____

2 Complete your project report.

OUR TREASURE HUNT

3 Present your report to your family and friends.

I can create a treasure hunt.

Review

1 Read and sort.

belt   earrings   find   follow   clues   lose   necklace   police
ring   search   sunglasses   thief   trainers   wristwatch

clothes and accessories	people	actions

2 Read and circle the correct words.

1. I ate / was eating my breakfast when they stole / were stealing my ring.
2. I ate / was eating a snack when they found / were finding my backpack.
3. What were you doing before you were falling / fell over?
4. I was playing / played volleyball when I was losing / lost my ring.
5. What was she doing when her shoe was breaking / broke ?
6. She wasn't running / didn't run when her shoe was breaking / broke .
7. What were they doing when they were seeing / saw the bird?
8. They were looking / looked at the clouds when they were seeing / saw the bird.
9. What was he doing when the man was running / ran in front of him?
10. He was following / followed a clue when the man was running / ran in front of him.

3 Read the secret message and write.

A	B	C	D	E	F	G	H	I	J	K	L	M	N	O	P	Q	R	S	T	U	V	W	X	Y	Z
z	y	x	w	v	u	t	s	r	q	p	o	n	m	l	k	j	i	h	g	f	e	d	c	b	a

BLF   ZIV   Z   TIVZG   WVGVXGREV

4 Write a secret message for your partner using the code in **3**.

_____

_____

Now go to your Progress Chart on page 4.

3 Checkpoint
UNITS 5 AND 6

1 🎧 **Listen and follow Alina's path.**

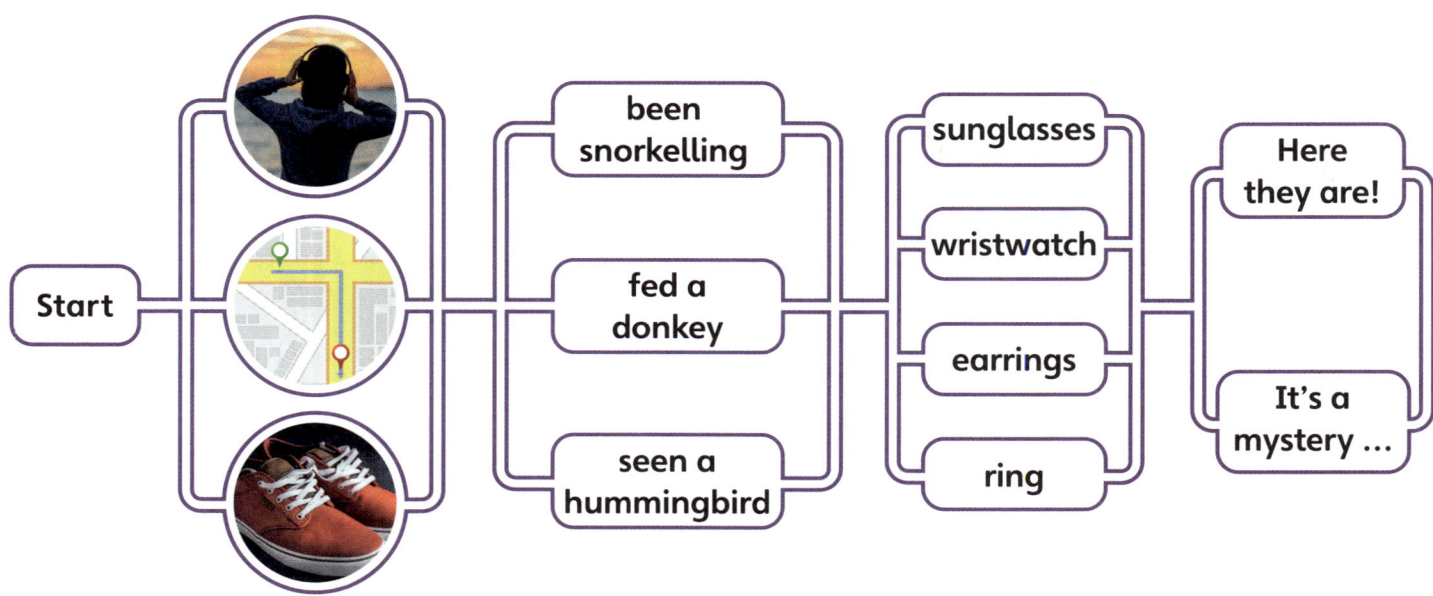

2 Listen again and tick ✓ the things Alina has done.

1 been snorkelling ☐
2 fed a donkey ☐
3 seen a hummingbird ☐
4 been to a desert island ☐
5 been camping ☐
6 been hiking ☐
7 been ziplining ☐
8 swum in the sea ☐
9 climbed up a tower ☐
10 walked on the beach ☐
11 visited a palace ☐
12 flown in a helicopter ☐

3 🌐 **Write a paragraph about something you have done. Share details of your experience.**

I have …

4 Read the article and circle T (True) or F (False).

Mystery thieves of Christmas Island

4 January

Christmas Island is a remote and beautiful island off the north coast of Australia. There are beaches for swimming and snorkelling, rainforests for hiking and spectacular waterfalls where tourists enjoy taking photographs.

However, the island was also home to a curious crime not long ago. Dr Helen Barnwell, a research scientist from London, visited the island to study a group of local marsupials called sugar gliders. One evening, she set up a special camera in the trees to photograph these interesting animals. But the next morning when she went to check her camera, it wasn't there. She looked around and saw some marks on the ground.

Local police officer Gloria Hann solved the mystery for Dr Barnwell. Officer Hann said, 'The local coconut crabs are the thieves. They have lived on the island for hundreds of years. They grab things they think are food and carry them away to their holes. We call them robber crabs!'

coconut crab

sugar glider

camera

1 Christmas Island is located off the south coast of Australia.   T / F
2 Dr Barnwell lives on Christmas Island.   T / F
3 She set her camera up in the morning.   T / F
4 Coconut crabs have lived on the island for many years   T / F
5 They are called robber crabs because they take things.   T / F

5 Put the words in order and write questions. Then ask a partner.

1 Have / a tablet / you / broken / ? / ever

_____

2 you / Have / ? / any / money / ever / found

_____

3 ever / ? / Have / you / lost / sunglasses / a pair of

_____

The Romans
CULTURE

1 Are these sports and games popular in your country? Have you ever seen or played any of them? Ask and answer.

hula hoop

car racing

chess

Hula hooping is popular in my country.
I've seen car racing.

I've played chess.
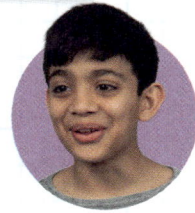

2 Read and number the pictures in order.

Ancient Romans loved sports. There were indoor and outdoor sports. A popular sport was hoop rolling. Ancient Roman children rolled their hoops by hitting them with a stick. They had races to see who could roll their hoop fastest.

Chariot racing was very popular, too. The chariots were pulled by horses. The charioteers drove their chariots 8.4 kilometres around an oval arena. They drove them very fast. The winner won a crown of leaves and a lot of money.

Ludus latrunculorum was an inside sport. It was a board game. Players practised military tactics. It was very popular because the Ancient Romans were great soldiers.

3 Which modern sports in **1** are like the Ancient Roman sports?

Chariot racing: _____   Hoop rolling: _____
Ludus latrunculorum: _____

4. Listen and complete.

> each other   gladiator events   most popular   stars today   the rich

Glorious Gladiators

Ancient Romans loved going to the amphitheatre to watch different events. **1** _____ _____ were one of the **2** _____ _____ sports in Ancient Rome, as well as chariot racing. Two gladiators fought **3** _____ _____ . They wore helmets and carried shields. Gladiators were very brave. **4** _____ _____ and the poor were gladiator fans. Everyone went to watch the events. Successful gladiators were loved and admired by Ancient Romans. They were like football, basketball and baseball **5** _____ _____ !

5. Read and circle the correct answers.

1. Gladiator events / Horse racing were the most popular sports in Ancient Rome.
2. Two / Three gladiators took part in the competition.
3. They were very brave / shy .
4. They had helmets and shields / boots and shields for protection.
5. No one / Everyone watched gladiator events.
6. They admired / were angry with the gladiators.

6. Imagine you are a Roman sportsperson. Write about your day.

I am a charioteer. Today I raced around the Colosseum. I won the race. Then I ...

I know about Ancient Romans.

7 What shall we eat?

How can we invent a lunch menu?

1 Complete the conversation. Then listen and check.

frozen yoghurt   haven't   mango   pineapple   sweet   would

Milkshake
• chocolate • strawberry •
• vanilla •

Frozen yoghurt
• Honey and nuts •
• Mango and pineapple •
• Kiwi and sweets •

Beatriz: What 1 _____ you like, Jimmy? A milkshake or a frozen yoghurt?

Jimmy: I'd like a 2 _____ _____ , please.

Beatriz: What kind?

Jimmy: 3 _____ and 4 _____ , please. I like fruit flavours.

Beatriz: Have you ever tried kiwi and sweets?

Jimmy: No, I 5 _____ . It sounds 6 _____ .

2 Solve the code. What is Cody asking for?

CODE CRACKER

| A | E | O | L | M | P | R | S |

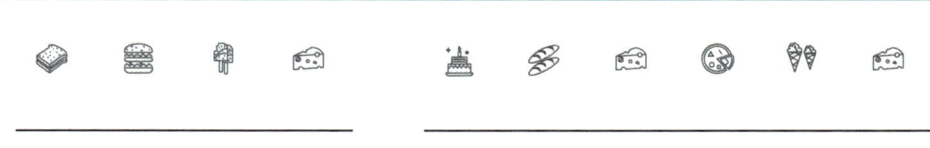

_____   _____ !

3 Play *Memory* in groups.

- I went to the shop and I bought … honey!
- I went to the shop and I bought honey and … apples!
- I went to the shop and I bought honey, apples and …

At the market

VOCABULARY

> I will learn words for food and cooking.

1  Look and write. Which things do you like cooking with?

1 s_____

2 s_____

3 v_____

4 h_____

5 f_____

6 o_____

2 Work in pairs. Look at the pictures in **1** for one minute. Then cover the pictures and test each other's memory.

- What's number 4?
- Umm … I think it's herbs.
- Yes, that's right.

3 Unscramble the words and complete the recipe for crepes.

LFURO   HNEOY   BUETTR   NTSU   GEG

HONEY AND NUT CREPES

- Mix 225 g of **1** _____ , one tablespoon of oil, 500 ml of milk and one **2** _____ in a bowl.
- Heat a pan. Add 15 ml of **3** _____ .
- Pour some of the crepe mixture into the hot pan and cook until bubbles form.
- Turn it over and cook it on the other side for one minute.
- Pour **4** _____ and sprinkle **5** _____ on top of the crepe, fold and serve.

I can use words for food and cooking.

Language lab

GRAMMAR: PRESENT PASSIVE

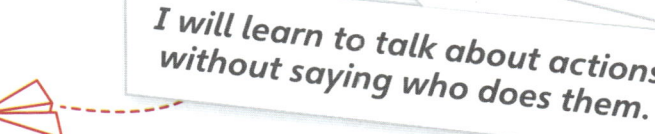

I will learn to talk about actions without saying who does them.

1 Complete the sentences with the correct form of the words in brackets.

1 Honey _____ (use) sometimes instead of sugar.
2 Yoghurt _____ (make) from milk.
3 Green tea _____ (drink) in China.
4 Peanuts _____ (grow) underground.
5 A lot of sushi _____ (eat) in Japan.

2 Write questions. Remember to use the past participle.

1 What / popcorn / make / from?
   _____?
2 How / milkshakes / make?
   _____?
3 Where / rice / grow?
   _____?
4 Where / salt / find?
   _____?

3 Read and number the pictures in the correct order.

From cocoa to chocolate

Chocolate is made from cocoa beans. Cocoa beans are found in pods on cacao trees.

The pods are opened. There are about 50 beans in each pod.

The beans are dried in the sun and they are sent to chocolate manufacturers all over the world.

The beans are crushed and mixed with milk and sugar.

Finally, the chocolate is heated and poured into moulds.

The finished chocolates are sent to shops and are sold. Then they are eaten by hungry people like you and me. Delicious!

4 Look at 3. Underline all the examples of present passive verbs.

5 Complete the information about candyfloss. Then listen and check.

> Candyfloss is very popular. It **1** _____ (make) from sugar, water, corn syrup and a little salt. Food colouring **2** _____ (use) to colour the candyfloss mixture blue, green, pink or yellow. The ingredients **3** _____ (heat), then spun around a stick. It is sold on street corners.

6 Read and number the steps in the correct order.

How Mexican Hot Chocolate is made.

a   First, milk is measured and warmed.

b   The milk and chocolate mixture are boiled and cinnamon is added.

c   Then chocolate is broken up and put into the warm milk.

d   Then the hot chocolate is poured into mugs. Marshmallows are not added to Mexican hot chocolate.

e   After the spice has been added, the mixture is stirred with a special whisk to add air.

7 Test your partner by asking them questions about candyfloss and hot chocolate.

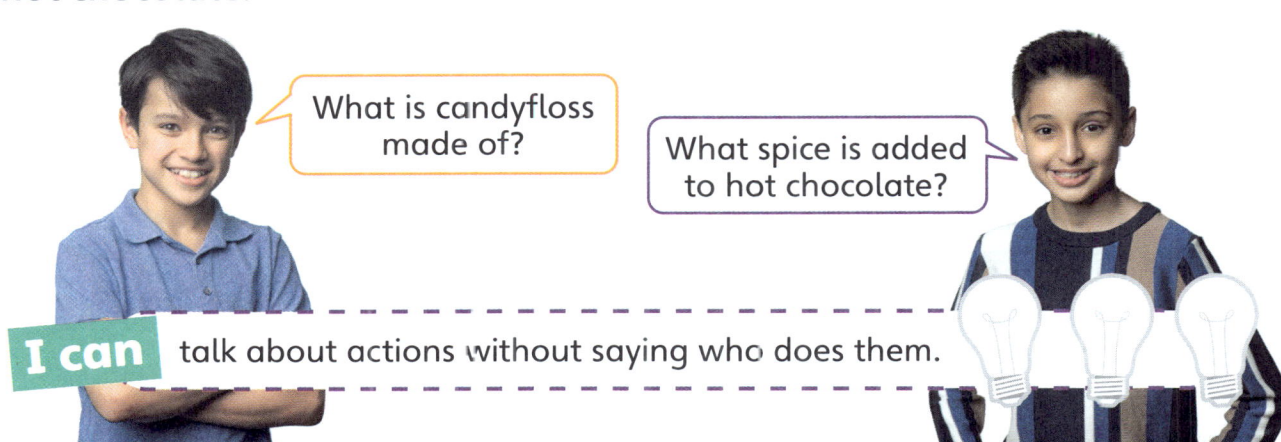

What is candyfloss made of?

What spice is added to hot chocolate?

I can talk about actions without saying who does them.

Story lab

READING

I will read a story about making soup.

1 Read *Tasty Soup* again. Then answer the questions.

1. What was Antonio's problem?
   Antonio was _____ .
2. Did the villagers want to help him at first?
   _____
3. What did Antonio do when he reached the stream?
   He _____ .
4. Who was the first person to help him?
   The first person to help him was _____ .
5. How did the villagers help him in the end?
   They _____ .
6. What did the villagers add to the meal at the end?
   They _____ .

2 Correct the false sentences.

1. Rosa was the first person to help Antonio.
   _____
2. Antonio wanted to make salad in his cooking pot.
   _____
3. The stone in the story was really magic.
   _____
4. The villagers brought fruit to Antonio.
   _____
5. They all ate the magic stone.
   _____
6. The final meal smelled disgusting.
   _____

3 Match the words to their meaning.

1	cooking pot	a	a liquid meal eaten with a spoon
2	stone	b	animal which is eaten as food
3	soup	c	hot food is made in it
4	herbs	d	a small piece of rock
5	beans	e	added to food to make it tasty
6	meat	f	pulses you can eat

4 Complete the sentences.

1 Antonio was looking for food because he was very _____ .
2 He tricked the villagers by telling them that the stone was _____ .
3 Antonio told one of the village women that the soup was a bit too _____ .
4 The soup smelled very good, but it wasn't _____ enough. Thanks to Rosa the problem was solved!
5 In the end the soup was delicious. Everyone said it was very _____ .

5 In groups, share your ideas about these questions. Give reasons for your answers.

Why do you think Antonio was so hungry?

What was Rosa like at the beginning of the story?

Why do you think Antonio added a stone to his pot of boiling water?

Was Antonio a good man or an untrustworthy man?

6 Read and solve the maths problems.

MATHS ZONE

If 4 villagers each add 3 ingredients to the soup, how many ingredients are added? _____

If each extra ingredient weighs 25 g, how much weight is added to the soup? _____

I can read a story about making soup.

Experiment lab

SCIENCE: SOLUTIONS AND MIXTURES

I will find out about solutions and mixtures.

1 Complete the sentences.

1. Sea water consists of _____ and water.
2. Salt is a _____ substance.
3. Sand is an _____ substance.
4. Sand and water mix but don't make a _____ .
5. Too much sugar or salt in foods is _____ .

> bad for you
> insoluble
> salt
> soluble
> solution

2 Answer the questions.

1. Why are fizzy drinks often unhealthy?
   _____

2. What happens when water is boiled?
   _____

3. What happens when sea water is boiled?
   _____

4. How can a mixture of water and sand be separated?
   _____

5. For a healthy diet, what advice should be followed?
   _____

3 Match the sentences to the pictures.

1. He's heating the mixture.
2. The water is bubbling in a pot.
3. He's putting a spoonful of salt into water.
4. He's mixing it and the salt is dissolving.
5. The water has evaporated and there is salt at the bottom of the pot.

4. **Work in pairs. Read these nutritional labels. Which is the healthier snack? Why?**

EXPERIMENT TIME

Report

1. **Write your report.**

   1. I washed and dried a glass. I checked that it was clean and completely dry.
   2. I filled the glass with warm water.
   3. I put a teaspoon of oil into the glass of warm water.
   4. I took a spoon and mixed the oil and water.
   5. I mixed it for 30 seconds. The oil did not dissolve.
   6. I mixed it for 30 more seconds. The oil still did not dissolve.
   7. My conclusion is that oil is insoluble.

2. **Continue your experiment. Use these substances. Record your results.**

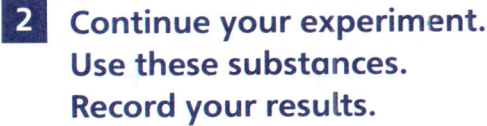

chalk

washing-up liquid

 about solutions and mixtures.

101

Ordering food

COMMUNICATION: *MUCH / MANY, ENOUGH*

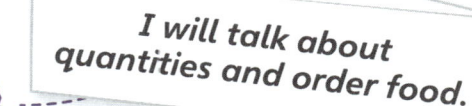

I will talk about quantities and order food.

1  Paul and his sister Nancy are buying food for a picnic. Listen and circle T (True) or F (False).

1. Nancy is very happy with the contents of the shopping trolley. T / F
2. Nancy says there's too much salt in crisps. T / F
3. Nancy asks Paul to put three apples in the trolley. T / F
4. Nancy wants to make cheese sandwiches for the picnic. T / F
5. They're meeting their friends in the garden. T / F

2 Look at the pictures. Talk about what Paul and Nancy said about the picnic.

> There are too many sandwiches.

3 In groups of three, role-play the conversation between the children who have arrived at the picnic and their friend Erin.

Nancy: Would you like a sandwich?
Erin: Yes, please.
Paul: Would you prefer a cheese and tomato sandwich or a chicken and lettuce sandwich?
Erin: Chicken and lettuce sounds delicious. I'll have one of those.
Paul: Here you are.
Erin: Have you got mayonnaise?
Nancy: Yes, here you are.
Erin: Thank you.

4 In groups of three, role-play a new conversation for you.

Would you like …?   Would you prefer …?   Have you got …?

I can talk about quantities and order food.

Writing lab

WRITING A RECIPE

I will write a recipe.

1 🔊 040 **Listen to the recipe and tick ✓ the ingredients you need.**

- ☐ apples
- ☐ bananas
- ☐ sugar
- ☐ honey
- ☐ eggs
- ☐ cream
- ☐ flour
- ☐ butter
- ☐ salt
- ☐ pepper
- ☐ coconut
- ☐ nuts
- ☐ milk

2 **Listen again and complete the recipe card.**

Banana muffins
Ingredients
3 large bananas
_____
_____
_____
_____
_____

3 **Complete the instructions for making banana muffins.**

> Add   Bake   Heat   Mix   Pour

1 _____ together the sugar, flour and salt.
2 _____ the butter in the microwave until it melts.
3 _____ the butter, egg and milk to the muffin mixture and mix.
4 _____ the mixture into a muffin tin.
5 _____ the muffins for 20 minutes at 180°C.

4 **Read the beginning of the story, then write the ending.**

It was Mitch's birthday. Six of his best friends were invited for a picnic in the garden. Mitch wanted to make mango muffins for the party. Mango muffins are made with mangoes, but Mitch didn't have enough mangoes in the house. There wasn't enough butter, either. So, Mitch took some money out of his piggy bank and
_____
_____
_____

I can write a recipe.

PROJECT AND REVIEW — UNIT 7

Invent a lunch menu

Project report

1 Complete the table.

What dishes did you include on your menu?		What did your menu look like? It had …	
☐ chicken	☐ fruit	☐ starters	☐ main courses
☐ vegetables	☐ ice cream	☐ desserts	☐ descriptions of food
☐ chocolate	☐ pizza	☐ ingredients	☐ clear writing
☐ nuts	☐ other	☐ decoration	
Did you role-play using your menu with another group?		**Did you role-play using another group's menu?**	
☐ They chose things from our menu.		☐ We chose things from their menu.	
☐ They wrote a review.		☐ We wrote a review.	
☐ We read reviews of our menu.		☐ They read our reviews.	
What did other groups say about your menu?			
They liked _____			
and _____ . They said _____ .			

2 Complete your project report. Use your dictionary to help you.

Report – Invent a lunch menu

First, we _____ .

Our menu _____ .

We role-played _____ .

They said our menu was _____ .

3 Share your report about the project with another group.

I can invent a lunch menu.

Review

1 Read and sort.

> flour herbs honey mango meat nuts oil pineapple
> salt spices strawberries sugar vegetables

pizza	ice cream

2 Write questions. Remember to use the past participle.

1 Where / rice / grow
   Where is rice grown?

2 What / ice cream / make of
   _____

3 What / spices / use for
   _____

4 How / doughnuts / cook
   _____

5 How long / pasta / cook for
   _____

6 What / cheese / make from
   _____

3 Complete the sentences with the correct form of the words in brackets.

1 Rice _____ (grow) in China.
2 Ice cream _____ (make) of cream, milk and sugar.
3 Spices _____ (use) for flavour.
4 Doughnuts _____ (drop) into hot oil.
5 Fresh pasta _____ (cook) for 2–3 minutes.

4 Jay and Liz are having a party, but Liz is worried. Circle the correct answers.

1 Have we got enough / too many food?
2 I think we've got too many / too much nuts.
3 We've got too many / too much ice cream.
4 We haven't got enough / too many pizzas.
5 Are there enough / too much bananas?

>>> Now go to your Progress Chart on page 4.

8 Our digital world

How can we create a song about technology?

1 Read and sort.

email   famous   guitar   headphones   keyboard   microphone
mobile phone   prize   screen   song   speaker   trumpet   website   winner

digital device	musical	contest

2 Unscramble the words to complete the sentences. Listen and check.

ETWIEBS
ORADYKEB
PCOMREOIHN
IGRTUA
GONS
HOSDHAENPE
BILMEO PHNEO
KSEREPA

CODE CRACKER

First, look up a songwriting 1 _____ online to learn how to write a song. Second, write lyrics for your 2 _____ . Next, get your 3 _____ or 4 _____ out and create music to go with your lyrics. Then connect your 5 _____ to your 6 _____ or 7 _____ and sing! Use your 8 _____ _____ to make a video of yourself singing your song. Play it back and watch yourself.

3 Add these words to the table in **1**.

compete   computer game   control   notes   songbook   text message

How do we use technology?

I will learn words to talk about technology.

VOCABULARY

1  **Complete the crossword.**

Across

2. something you can win in a competition or a race
4. an electronic musical instrument that is like a piano
5. a page on the internet where you can find information about something
6. a word meaning 'known by many people'
8. a short piece of music with words that you sing
9. a devise that you wear over your ears to listen to the radio or music

Down

1. a musical instrument with six strings that you play with your fingers
3. something you can ring your friends on
7. the part of television or computer where you can see images or information

2  **Complete the chant. Listen and check. Then recite the chant.**

download   listen   look up   record   use

I use my devices every day.
I use my computer in many ways.
Press a button. Check a site.
Send an email. What to write?
I use my devices every day.
I **1** _____ my tablet in many ways.
2 _____ to music. **3** _____ apps.
4 _____ a message. **5** _____ maps.

3  **Write a new verse about mobile phones.**

I use my devices every day.
I use my mobile phone in many ways.

I can use words to talk about technology.

Language lab

GRAMMAR: QUESTION TAGS

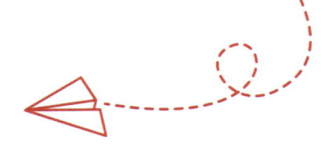

I will check information using question tags.

1 Read and circle the correct tags.

1. This computer game is great, is it? / **isn't it?** / isn't she?
2. We can't use this tablet to take photos, **can we?** / can't we? / can they?
3. You like playing the violin, do they? / do you? / **don't you?**
4. These magazines aren't very interesting, **are they?** / aren't they? / isn't it?
5. I'm not early, am I? / can I? / **aren't I?**

2 Complete the sentences with the correct tags. Then listen and check.

1. Mary can ride a horse, _____ .
2. The bus comes at 7:00, _____ .
3. Your sister isn't in our class, _____ .
4. Tomorrow is your birthday, _____ .
5. They taste like peaches, _____ .

3 Do the general knowledge quiz. Circle the correct answers.

Quiz

1 Salt and sugar are soluble, aren't they?
Yes, they are. / No, they aren't.

2 The process of separating a soluble solution is filtration, isn't it?
Yes, it is. / No, it isn't.

3 A binary code uses two numbers, doesn't it?
Yes, it does. / No, it doesn't.

4 Hummingbirds live in Antarctica, don't they?
Yes, they do. / No, they don't.

5 Some animators use computers to make animations, don't they?
Yes, they do. / No, they don't.

6 Two out of three is a quarter, isn't it?
Yes, it is. / No, it isn't.

7 The capital city of France is London, isn't it?
Yes, it is. / No, it isn't.

4 Put the words in order and make sentences with question tags. Match and write them under the pictures. Then say the answers.

a strong / they / aren't / are / they
b don't / they / look / delicious / they
c red / she's / hasn't / got / hair / she
d play / loves / he / football / doesn't / to / he

_____   _____   _____   _____
_____   _____   _____   _____
_____   _____   _____   _____

5 Complete the questions. Then ask and answer with a partner.

1 You _____ in the Year 5, aren't you?
2 You like chocolate, _____ ?
3 You _____ ill today, are you?
4 You _____ play volleyball, do you?

6 Look at the picture and make some guesses about the person. Use question tags.

Age: She's _____ years old, isn't she?
Nationality: She's _____ , isn't she?
Sport: She loves _____ , _____ ?
Favourite gadget: It's her _____ _____ ?
Favourite place: It's the _____ _____ ?

7 Now listen and check your guesses in 6.

I can check information using question tags.

Story lab

READING

I will read a story about a competition.

THE COMPETITION

1 Read *The Competition* again. Number the events in the correct order.

a Lily and Tyler noticed a poster about a walking competition. ☐
b Tyler and Lily checked the big screen in the town square. ☐
c Lily was disappointed she was losing so she went home. ☐
d The screen showed that Lily didn't have as many points as Tyler. ☐
e They downloaded an app to count their steps. ☐
f During the competition, they walked thousands of steps every day. ☐
g Tyler went to Lily's house and discovered that she was cheating. ☐

2 Read and circle T (True) or F (False).

1 The app is downloaded onto a mobile phone. T / F
2 The app records time. T / F
3 The app sends information to be displayed on a big screen. T / F
4 The person who has walked the fewest steps is the winner. T / F
5 Tyler wasn't good at many things. T / F
6 Lily was good at many things. T / F

3 Tick ✓ the conversation that matches the picture. Discuss why with a partner.

a ☐ 'You like walking, don't you?' asked Lily.
'Yes, I do', answered Tyler. 'Let's enter. It won't be easy, but I think it will be fun!'

b ☐ 'Look!' shouted a little boy, 10 minutes later.
'Lily's score is going up really fast.'
'Look! She's done 57,300 steps … no, 57,400 …'
'You're kidding.'

c ☐ 'Oh, Lily', he said. 'The app thought you were walking.'
'Sorry', said Lily. 'I was cheating. I wanted to win. It was silly.'

4 Punctuate the conversation. Use quotation marks (''), commas (,), question marks (?) and full stops (.).

You like engineering don't you Tyler asked Lily
Yes I do answered Lily
There's a competition in town next week said Tyler
Let's enter it! exclaimed Lily excitedly

5 Read and solve the maths problems.

MATHS ZONE

Abby entered the same walking competition as Tyler and Lily. The first day she walked 6920 steps, the second day she walked 7000 steps and the third day she walked 4080 steps.

1 How many steps did Abby walk altogether? _____

2 What was the average number of steps she walked a day? _____

3 How many more steps will she need to reach 20,000? _____

6 Circle the correct tags. Then ask and answer about the story with a partner.

1 Lily is embarrassed, is she / isn't she ? Why?

2 It isn't good to cheat, is it / isn't it ? Why?

3 Tyler is a good friend, is he / isn't he ? Why?

I can read a story about a competition.

Experiment lab

SCIENCE: HOW DOES ELECTRICITY WORK?

I will find out about electricity.

1 Do the quiz. Circle a or b.

1 Electricity is a type of …
   a energy.
   b artificial light.

2 The two kinds of energy are …
   a static and lightning.
   b static and current.

3 Static electricity sometimes forms in …
   a clouds.
   b circuits.

4 Some appliances use ____ electricity.
   a static
   b current

5 Other appliances use …
   a batteries.
   b lightning.

6 To power an electrical device, you need a/an …
   a off switch.
   b circuit.

2 Look at the appliances and tick ✓ the ones you've got at home.

hair dryer

TV

TV remote control

washing machine

remote control helicopter

lamp

3 Work with a partner to guess the form of energy the appliances in **2** use: electrical current (plug in) or batteries (including rechargeable). Then check at home.

> The hairdryer uses an electrical current, doesn't it?

> Yes, it does. The remote control doesn't use electrical current, does it? I think it uses batteries.

4 Choose one of the appliances in **2**. How would your life be different without it?

Our washing machine is very useful. We often use it at my house. We need the washing machine to wash our clothes when they are dirty. The washing machine uses electricity to make movement to wash the clothes. Without a washing machine we would have to wash our clothes by hand. I like the washing machine.

EXPERIMENT TIME

Report

1 What did you learn from your experiment?

I learnt _____ _____ .

2 Did your experiment work? Write the reasons you think your experiment succeeded or failed.

My experiment   worked / failed   because _____ _____ .

 how an electrical circuit works.

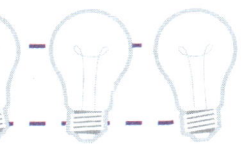

Music and games

COMMUNICATION: -ING OR -ED?

I will describe things and say how things make me feel.

1 Unscramble the feelings and complete the sentences.

> REDBO   EXITEDC   FRINEDGHTE   INSTTEEDER   RELEDAX

1 When I'm about to do something new for the first time, I feel _____ .
2 When I do my deep breathing exercises, I feel _____ .
3 During a very long film that I'm not interested in, I feel _____ .
4 When someone is teaching me something I want to know, I'm very _____ .
5 When I'm alone in the dark, I feel _____ .

2 🎧 045 Complete. Then listen and check.

1 I'm falling asleep. This film is so _____ .

2 That Halloween mask is very _____ .

3 The final minutes of a game are often _____ .

4 Listening to the sounds of the sea is very _____ .

5 Science is much more _____ than Maths.

3 Read and circle the correct words.

a Dad is interested / interesting in the TV programme.
b Alan thinks the show is frightened / frightening .
c Mum thinks the show is excited / exciting .

a The children are bored / boring .
b The programme they are watching is very bored / boring .
c They need a more excited / exciting programme.

I can describe things and say how things make me feel.

Writing lab

WRITING A STORY FROM PICTURES

> I will write a story about some pictures.

1 Look and write sentences to describe the pictures.

> beach   brother   children   cousin   cry   dog   drop   eat   exciting
> happy   holiday   ice cream   lick   relaxed   relaxing   sad   sister

1 *The dog looks hungry.*
2 *The children are eating ice cream.*
3 ___
4 ___
5 ___
6 ___
7 ___
8 ___

2 Draw a storyboard for your story.

One day	Suddenly	Then	In the end

3 Write the story and add more details.

___
___
___

4  Work in pairs. Share your stories.

I can write a story about some pictures.

PROJECT AND REVIEW — UNIT 8

Create a song about technology

Project report

1 Complete the table.

What was your song about?	What sounds did you use in your song?
☐ tablet ☐ apps ☐ computer ☐ headphones ☐ mobile phone ☐ other	☐ clicking fingers ☐ clapping hands ☐ stomping ☐ pencils on desks ☐ scraping chairs ☐ other
What rhythms did you use in your song?	**What symbols did you use for your score?**
☐ fast and exciting ☐ slow and relaxing	☐ asterisks ☐ stars ☐ wavy lines ☐ other
Did you practise your song? ☐ Yes ☐ No	**What did other groups like about your song?** They liked _____ and _____ .

2 Complete your project report.

What was your song about? _____

What sounds did you use in your song? _____

What rhythms did you use in your song? _____

What symbols did you use for your score? _____

Did you practise your song? Yes ☐ No ☐

What did other groups like about your song?

They liked _____ and _____ .

3 Share your report about the project with another group. Check others' reports using question tags.

I can create a song about technology.

Review

1 Find and circle the words from the unit.

B	M	O	B	I	L	E	P	H	O	N	E	A	T	P
A	P	P	O	C	O	M	K	E	Y	B	O	A	R	D
N	U	T	J	E	R	K	E	A	B	Y	A	O	U	O
D	R	D	Y	M	T	R	U	D	M	P	E	T	M	W
G	U	G	U	I	T	A	R	P	G	U	I	I	P	N
S	D	A	T	C	O	L	P	H	U	R	A	I	E	L
C	E	N	E	R	U	P	L	O	A	D	E	R	T	O
R	R	N	S	O	S	P	E	N	K	A	S	P	E	A
C	E	L	L	P	S	C	R	E	E	N	L	P	H	D
O	M	N	E	H	C	F	G	S	P	E	A	K	E	R
C	O	M	C	O	M	P	U	T	E	R	R	U	M	P
K	B	E	Y	N	M	I	C	R	C	E	A	P	P	H
O	N	E	M	E	I	C	K	B	O	A	S	T	A	P

app
band
computer
download
guitar
headphones
keyboard
microphone
mobile phone
screen
speaker
trumpet
upload

2 Solve the riddles.

1. I speak into it to make my voice louder. I sing into it with my band. _____
2. I use it to write on my computer. I play music with it. _____
3. I download music onto it. I use it to ring my mum. _____
4. I plug them into my mobile phone. I can hear well with them. _____
5. It's a musical instrument. It's got six strings. I play it in a band. _____
6. It's flat. I can see things on it. My computer, phone and tablet have got one. _____

3 Complete the sentences with question tags.

1. A singer uses a microphone, _____ _____ ?
2. We can send text messages on our mobile phones, _____ _____ ?
3. Some people use websites to help write their songs, _____ _____ ?
4. She isn't famous, _____ _____ ?
5. The contest is tomorrow, _____ _____ ?

>> Now go to your Progress Chart on page 4.

4 Checkpoint
UNITS 7 AND 8

1 🎧 046 **Listen and follow the path.**

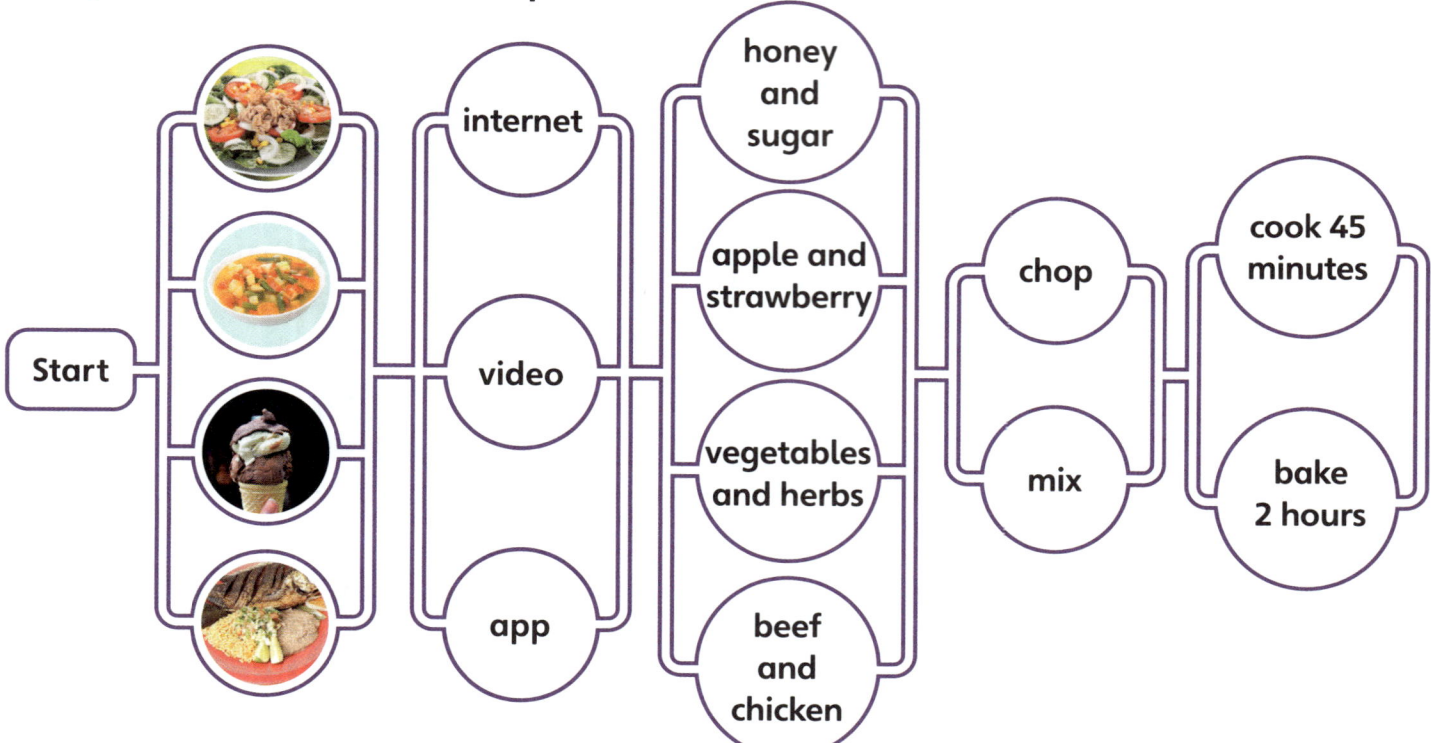

2 Read the questions and match them to the correct answer.

a How much butter do we need?
b What are we going to make today?
c Where did you find the recipe?
d What ingredients do we need?
e How long does it take?

1 _____
Let's make cornbread. I've got a great new recipe!

2 _____
I looked it up on the internet.

3 _____
Fresh corn, butter, salt, milk and eggs.

4 _____
It says we need about 110 g.

5 _____
It says it takes about 10 minutes to prepare and 25 minutes to bake.

3 Read and circle.

1 Avocados are grown in
  a Mexico.
  b Antarctica.
2 92% of avocados are grown in
  a Michoacán.
  b Oaxaca.
3 Avocados are used to make
  a milkshakes.
  b guacamole.
4 340 kilograms are produced every year by
  a one avocado farm.
  b one avocado tree.
5 Most avocados are imported by
  a the United States.
  b China.

4 Work in pairs. Ask and answer questions about the information in 3.

5 Write everything you have eaten today in the table. Then discuss it with a partner.

| Write the food and the amount. | Keep a record for the coming week. | Have you got a healthy diet? | How could you change your diet? |

fruit and nuts	vegetables and oils	grains

meat	sugar	dairy

Celebrating festivals
CULTURE

1 Read and complete the information sheet.

In India, people love festivals. There are a lot of festivals every year. In fact, there are more than 30. And Indian festivals are a lot of fun. For example, there is Holi festival in March. The Holi festival is also called the Festival of Colours. This festival says goodbye to winter and welcomes the spring. It's a time for people to meet, play, laugh and forget old fights and arguments.

How do people celebrate the Holi festival? They throw paint powder and coloured water all over each other. The paint powder and coloured water symbolise happiness and the arrival of brightly coloured spring flowers. The Holi festival is a magical time in India.

Name of festival: _____
Month of festival: _____
Its popular name: _____
What it celebrates: _____
How it is celebrated: _____
_____

2 In groups, talk about a festival in your country.

When is it?

Are there any special foods/drinks?

How do you celebrate?

Do people wear special clothes or a costume?

3 Write four sentences about a festival you enjoy in your country.

_____
_____
_____
_____

4 🎧 047 **Listen and circle T (True) or F (False).**

1. Jaipur is a city in the south of India. T / F
2. In India, elephants represent kings and queens for many people. T / F
3. The Elephant festival takes place in autumn. T / F
4. At the festival, elephants are decorated with coloured flowers. T / F
5. The best decorated elephant wins a prize. T / F
6. Elephants take part in sports events at the festival. T / F

5 Correct the false statements in 4.

_____
_____
_____

6 💬 In pairs, decide on a festival to hold where you live. When is it? What does it celebrate? Do people eat special food and wear special clothes? Do they dance, sing or do special activities? Look at the photos for ideas.

sweet biscuits and other food

special candles

fireworks

7 🎨 **Design a poster to advertise the festival you created in 6.**

Time: Place: Cost: Activities:

I know about different festivals.

Extra writing

Unit 1

1 Write silly instructions using **must**, **must not**, **have to** and **don't have to**. Choose from the suggestions or use your own ideas.

- How to be a bad student.
- How to be a terrible dog owner.
- How to be an annoying neighbour.

> How to be a bad student.
> You must arrive late.
> You must never do your homework.

Unit 2

1 Match the poems to the pictures.

a A pointy, yellow star, shining brightly in the sky.

b An exciting small red flower in the desert. It pushes up from the hot ground.

c A cool, soft and round raindrop. It splashes on the hot pavement. Sizzle! Sizzle!

2 Choose a word and write it in the centre of the spidergram. Then write as many describing words around it as you can think of.

cloud   desert   lake   pyramid   raindrop   river   rock   snow   waterfall

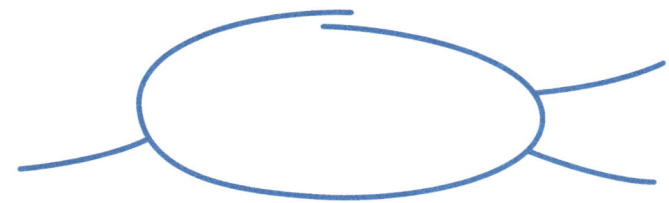

3 Write a shape poem with your ideas in 2.

Unit 3

Extra writing

1 Imagine your project festival is happening this weekend. Write notes about what is happening at the festival.

2 Write an email to invite a friend to the festival. Write about the activities, the food, the people, the music and the shows at the festival.

Hi _____ !
I'm going to the _____ festival this weekend. Do you want to come?
This is the plan:
_____
_____
_____
_____
Next, _____
After that, _____
Finally, _____
Say you will come!
From,

Extra writing

Unit 4

1 Complete the profile for your favourite actor.

Name: _____
Nationality: _____
Age: _____
Most famous films: _____
Characters played: _____
Best performance: _____

2 Write a paragraph about your favourite actor.

Unit 5

1 Read the information about Kenya and tick ✓ what you want to do.

Nairobi, Kenya

Full-day tours: ☐ Safari: See rhinos, lions, zebras   ☐ Mountain trip: Hike up Mt Longonot
Half-day tours: ☐ City visit   ☐ Zoo: Feed giraffes, elephants

2 Answer the questions a journalist sent you.

Where are you now? _____
_____

What have you done today? _____
_____

Why do you enjoy travelling? _____
_____

Where would you like to go next? _____
_____

3 Swap your answers in **2** with a partner. Write an article about your partner's travels.

Extra writing

Unit 6

1 Write a diary entry about the last time you lost something.

2 Use one of the codes in Unit 6 to write about how you felt.

3 Share your secret message with a partner. Can your partner work out the message?

Extra writing

Unit 7

1 Think about a recipe and answer the question.

What do you want to cook?
_____

2 Write a list of ingredients you will need.

3 Write instructions for making your dish.

> add   bake   cook   dip   eat   fill   heat   mix   pour   shape

1 _____
2 _____
3 _____
4 _____
5 _____
6 _____

4 Draw your dish.

Extra writing

Unit 8

1 Look at the pictures. Think and write notes about what happened.

> Terrible. Listening to music. Using my best friend's tablet, computer and headphones. Having fun. Feeling excited.

2 Imagine you are telling the story. Write about what happened.

_____
_____
_____
_____
_____
_____
_____

3 Work in pairs. Share your stories.

What happened in your story?

In my story, a lot of exciting things happened …

Pearson Education Limited
KAO TWO
KAO Park
Hockham Way
Harlow, Essex
CM17 9SR
England

and Associated Companies throughout the world.

english.com/englishcode

© Pearson Education Limited 2021

All rights reserved; no part of this publication may be reproduced, stored in a retrieval system, or transmitted in any form or by any means, electronic, mechanical, photocopying, recording, or otherwise without the prior written permission of the Publishers.

First published 2021
Ninth impression 2025

ISBN: 978-1-292-32283-4

Set in Heinemann Roman 12 pt
Printed in Slovakia by Neografia

Acknowledgements
The publishers and author(s) would like to thank the following people and institutions for their feedback and comments during the development of the material:

Argentina
Maria Belen Gonzalez Milbrandt (Director Colegio Sol De Funes), Alejandra Garre (Coordinator Colegio San Patricio), Patricia Bettucci (Teacher Colegio Verbo Encarnado), Colegio Los Arroyos (Coordinator Luciana Pittondo), Instituto Stella Maris (Coordinator Ana Maria Ferrari), Gabriela Dichiara (Coordinator Nivel Pre-Primario En Escuela Normal N° 1 Dr Nicolas Avellaneda), Alejandra Ferreyra & Maria Elena Casals (Profesor Escuela Normal N° 1 Dr Nicolas Avellaneda), Maria Julia Occhi (Primary Director Colegio San Bartolomé Sede Fisherton), Gisele Manzur (English Director- Colegio Educativo Latinoamericano), Griselda Rodriguez (Ex-Directora de Instituto IATEL), Cultural Inglesa de Santa Fe (Olga Poloni y Silvia Cantero), Escuela Primaria de la Universidad Nacional del Litoral (Santa Fe) (Ricardo Noval, Natalia Mártirez y Romina Papini), Colegio La Salle Jobson Santa Fe (Santa Fe) (Miriam Ibañez), Colegio de la Inmaculada Concepción (Santa Fe) (Gabriela Guglielminetti), Colegios Niño Jesús y San Ezequiel Moreno (Santa Fe) (Ivana Serrano), Advice Prep School (Santa Fe) (Virginia Berutti), Centro de Enseñanza de Inglés Mariana G. Puygros (Santa Fe). Focus Group Participants: Alejandra Aguirre (Coordinator Colegio Español), Alicia Ercole (Director Instituto CILEL (Casilda)), Marianella Robledo (Coordinator Insituto CILEL (Casilda)), Viviana Valenti (Director Instituto Let's Go), Natalia Berg (Prof. Colegio de La Paz (San Nicolás)).

Turkey
Ugur Okullari, Isik Okullari, Doğa Koleji, Fenerbahce Koleji, Arı Okullari, Maya Okullari, Yükselen Koleji, Pinar Koleji, Yeşilköy Okullari, Final Okullari, Vizyon Koleji

Image Credits:
123RF.com: adrianhancu 112, Aleksandr Frolov 69, Andriy Dovzhykov 68, Antonio Guillem 75, auremar 86, badmanproduction 90, bogumil 28, Cathy Yeulet 41, 58, 62, cfweng 121, Chelsie Bakken 79, Chon Kit Leong 66, claudiodivizia 12, domenicogelermo 27, dotshock 12, Elangovan Munuswamy Vaiyapuri 69, Fernando Gregory Milan 79, Graham Oliver 39, Hermant Mehta 120, Inspirestock International - Exclusive Contributor 39, Izflzf 86, Jan Miks 95, khosrork 109, kletr 112, Kzenon 81, lightwise 17, Marcos Castillo 97, Mikkel Bigandt 92, milkos 111, Nadexda Murmakova 66, nazarnj 122, neyro2008 38, Nikhil Gangavane 121, PA©ter Gudella 80, picsfive 17, Prapan Ngawkeaw 34, Robyn Mackenzie 17, Rolando Da Jose 84, Rommel Canlas 58, Ruth Black 109, Shannon Fagan 62, Somchai Jongmeesuk 122, Steve Byland 73, Steven Prorak 34, Vladimir Rublev 127, 127, Vladimir Volkov 92, zerbor 78; **Getty Images:** Robert Daly 92, SolStock 40, Stuart Dee 81; **Pearson Education Asia Ltd:** Coleman Yuen 22, Joey Chan 38; **Pearson Education Ltd:** Jon Barlow 21, 29, 35, 35, 38, 41, 43, 46, 57, 63, 68, 86, 92, 97, 99, 113, 120, 127, Jules Selmes 58, 81, 86; **Shutterstock:** 36, 105, 839950 115, aerogondo2 93, Africa Studio 103, Air Images 114, Alexander Trinitatov 58, AmaPhoto 112, ampFotoStudio 118, Andresr 39, Andrew Haddon 111, Andrew Zarivny 16, Andriy Popov 109, Anibal Trejo 25, ANK46. 34, antb 58, Anton Veselov 17, Aris Suwanmalee 8, Art Neli 78, Baptist 79, Birdiegal 68, Blend Images 81, Bob Alex 64, Bouybin 73, Brent Hofacker 37, Burlingham 13, C Levers 95, Chris Burt 91, Chris Harvey 28, covenant 74, Damir Khabirov 112, Daxiao Productions 13, Denis Belitsky 66, Drew Horne 73, ESB Professional 12, espies 121, Eugene Sergeev 91, Gelpi JM 7, Goldilock Project 36, Goncharov_Artem 39, gpointstudio 28, hispan 91, Indigo Fish 78, isaac jose sanchez meza 64, Iurii Davydov 74, javarman 74, jaxT 28, jonson 112, KateStone 86, Kiselev Andrey Valerevich 52, Kudryashka 121, Kzenon 86, Leah-Anne Thompson 81, lightpoet 66, Lillac 22, lowpower225 34, Lukas Gojda 2, M. Unal Ozmen 95, Manuel Fernandes 39, Marina Shanti 95, Mark Poprocki 58, marketa1982 28, Maryna Kulchytska 17, masisyan 38, Mercury Green 78, Micolas 37, Mnyjhee 23, Moises Fernandez Acosta 95, Monika Wisniewska 66, MZPHOTO. CZ 73, Nattakorn_Maneerat 62, Nikitina Olga 17, Noam Armonn 30, Olena Tur 75, Operation Shooting 24, orientalprincess 118, Patrick Poendl 75, paula french 124, Peeter Kim 118, Pete Pahham 109, photomaster 73, Picsfive 115, Piyawat Nandeenopparit 78, PongMoji 13, Poprotskiy Alexey 90, Radu Bercan 90, robert cicchetti 66, Roman Yanushevsky 122, rook76 112, schankz 73, Sebastian Knight 73, Shulevskyy Volodymyr 95, siamionau pavel 118, Snap Happy 28, souayang kanxao 94, steliangagiu 93, Steve Mann 73, StockImageFactory.com 115, 115, Svetlana Foote 78, Switlana Sonyashna 81, Tim Large 79, Tretyakov Viktor 39, tusharkoley 22, VaLiza 27, Valua Vitaly 109, vitmore 13, Vixit 22, wavebreakmedia 12, 114, Wesley Lazarus 7

All other images © Pearson Education

Video screenshots:
Jungle Creative

Illustrated by:
Anita Barghigiani/Astound US pp.98; Scott Burroughs/IllustrationOnline pp.9; Jay Carter pp.11, 19, 45, 83 (bottom), 96, 101 (bottom), 102; Julia Castaño/The Bright Agency pp.3, 70; Andrea Castro Naranjo/Beehive Illustration pp.32, 50-51, 72 ,80; Maria Luisa Di Gravio/Astound US pp.110 (bottom), 111; Ria Maria Lee/The Bright Agency pp.14; Leesh Li/Beehive Illustration pp.26-27; Isabel Muñoz/The Bright Agency pp.54; Maria Perera/Astound US pp.23, 24, 39, 42-43, 71, 92, 100, 101 (top), 110 (top), 113; Ana Sebastian/Sylvie Poggio Artists pp.83 (top); Joseph Wilkins/Beehive Illustration pp.4-5.

Cover Image: Front: **Pearson Education Ltd:** Jon Barlow